Yes We Can

Yes We Can

Savings We Can Believe In

VILLY CHOUTE

The Bailout the People Need . . .

To order additional copies of this book, contact:
Xlibris Corporation
1-888-795-4274
www.Xlibris.com
Orders@Xlibris.com
57743

CONTENTS

Preface

Economists, reporters, bankers, multi-millionaires, lawmakers, and leaders around the world all weigh in on how to save the planet from an economic disaster. Every major business around the world worries about their nest egg and begins to use fear to receive financial assistance, allowing these businesses to further their lavish lifestyles. These businesses convincingly make the case; if they fail, the impact would be catastrophic. Governments around the world are now in a state of panic and are willing to provide these businesses whatever they need to remain open. For instance, the U.S. government utilizes the *peoples'* tax dollars to bailout these corporate malfeasance and hope they will pass on the profit. This is *trickle-down theory*, and it has failed the people. This has been the promise made by most of these corporate giants to governments around the world. You provide us with incentives to build out our institutions; we will then employ your citizens. All we've seen is the rich are getting richer and the poor are becoming poorer. Everyone wants a drastic plan to save the economy, but the decision makers are all part owners in giant corporations or have some indirect interest in these companies. One can understand how difficult it is for political leaders to keep in open mind.

Every major plan put forth targets the creation of jobs. It seems at this point in time that giving the *peoples'* tax money to these corporations for various projects that will create jobs is a risk we cannot afford. Allow the *people* to present their own drastic plan. We recognize the importance of job creation in an ailing economy, however, this is not all. The Bailout the people need is to adjust the mortgage amortization schedule that currently creates more wealth for the wealthy and erodes our savings. The Bailout the People Need is to modernize the education system and create sound wealth management tools. We cannot trust a system that takes advantage of us, taking away most of our savings due to necessities. We can drill ourselves out of the mortgage mess, but real reform is necessary.

Introduction

Since the inception of mortgage loans, mortgage institutions have used the system of amortization to recover invested capital from home financing considered as risky investments. Lending institutions view home financing investments as a major risk because of the nature of the process to reclaim the property in case of a default by the homeowner and the period this money is unavailable. For this simple fact, we pay a hefty price to keep a roof over our heads. Thus the amortization system uses a method where over 75% of the mortgagors' monthly mortgage payment goes toward mortgage loan interest for more than half the maturity date of the mortgage note. Conversely, over 90% of the monthly payment collected by the mortgagee goes toward mortgage loan interest within the first seven years of the loan. This creates a situation where a home purchased in a market like today (over a seven-year period) becomes almost unmarketable, unless one is able to contribute a large down payment at the time of purchase. This method concentrates most of the mortgage interest up front, and the principal toward the end of mortgage term. Most economists agree that we will never see a real estate market like this again where property values literally double over six months to a year's time. It is even unlikely to experience 3%-5% increase yearly over the next five to seven years. Given the uncertainty of the market or its dubious future (whereas the average household income's falling as workers settle for pay cuts). Most mortgagors will see more than 50% of their income go toward their homes, despite the fact that average home prices are also down.

This will leave us with very little money for our kids' college and our retirement. In the past, we mortgaged the education for our kids in the quest for a fresh start after graduation. Now these kids would have to get education loans to pay for their schools, amassing a large financial burden given the cost of tuition today. In this book we are going to make the case for the bailout we need, which will produce *savings* we can believe in. Yes, we can! My bailout vision consists of the following:

1. Forbid salary discrimination in the workplace and enforce an even pay distribution for equal work in the workforce.
2. Forgive last two years consumers' debts through government debt settlements with creditors to improve credit rating.
3. Adjust amortization schedule to allow more loan principal pay down in the early years of the mortgage, thus building up real savings.
4. Outlaw daily interest compounding by credit card companies. Require credit card companies to compound interest quarterly and increase monthly payments.
5. The Tax code of the United States should be modified to make rent payment a taxable deduction just like mortgage interest.
6. Improve standards of living in neighboring countries within the Americas to improve product export and reduce U.S. business' astronomical expansion costs to distanced countries like China and India.
7. Raise the education standards of high school students requiring the acquisition of necessary skills to prevent a repeat of high school-level classes in college.
8. Provide more incentives to students that major in science and technology to ensure that technical skills are not outsourced, thereby reducing our dependence on foreign workers.
9. Government should reduce their interest in profit-making investments. This creates a conflict of interest and puts the security of the peoples' investment at risk.
10. Prohibit a company to get so big that it cannot fail through competition and is immune to enforcement of the antitrust laws.

Chapter 1

INCOME

Income in its purest form is any money received through any source possible. For most of us during our lifetime, our income will come from being an employee and self-employed. No one system can manage to fully assess the actual income of an individual or a company. The system is at the mercy of its citizens and entrepreneurs to report its income accordingly. Income data in America, in my opinion, is very unreliable and not a reflection of the true issue as the Internal Revenue Service (IRS) battles against tax evasion. The U.S. Census Bureau revealed the annual median income in the United States in 2006 was about $43,000. As we analyze this data further into different races as depicted in figure 1, it is found that the annual median income of Asian Americans was $58,000, Whites was $48,000, Hispanic Americans was $34,000, and Black Americans was $30,000. I used this year's data to illustrate a point. The housing market was nearly at its peak in 2006 until it began to disintegrate very rapidly in the subsequent years.

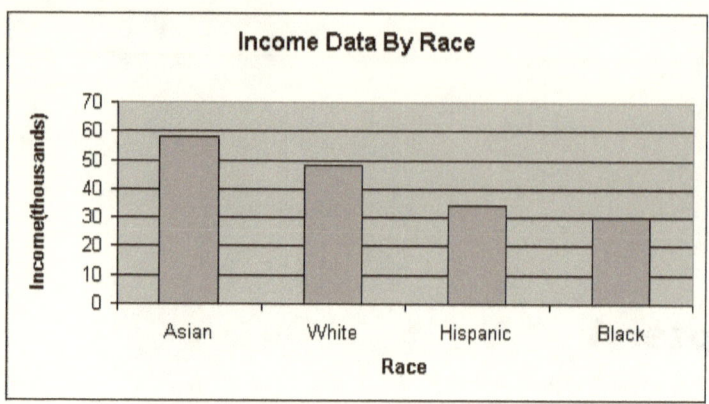

Fig. 1

In 2006, data shows 90% of Americans had an annual income of less than $100,000, which meant most Americans were unqualified to purchase a home in the range of $350,000 (using the available government mortgage guidelines). The other 10% made purchases above their means in an attempt to take advantage of tax savings of mortgage interests. Figure 2 and figure 3 below illustrated the tax liability at 28% and 33% tax brackets for a single person, a married couple, and someone with at least a dependent (head of household or single parents). The Internal Revenue Service (IRS) collects over $100,000 of taxes from a single person making roughly $350,000 per year, $98,000 from a head of household and $94,000 from a married couple at the 33% tax bracket. At this level, your income after federal taxes is approximately $250,000 a year (without factoring in social security and Medicare taxes).

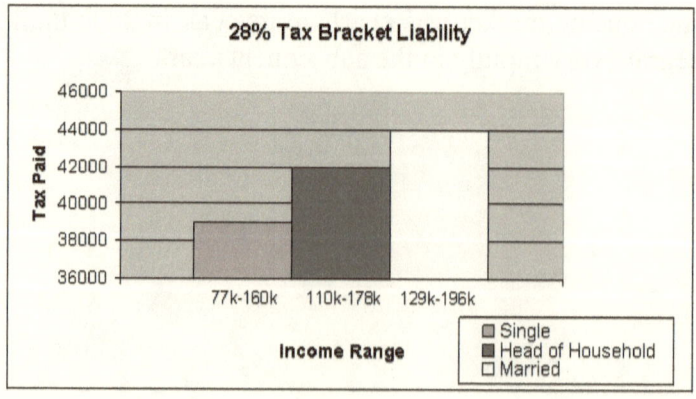

Fig. 2

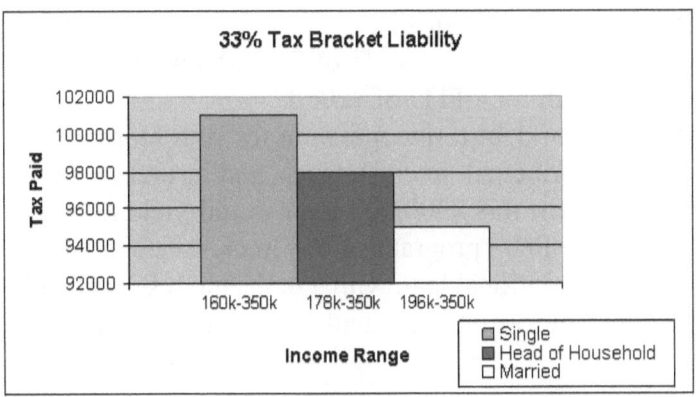

Fig. 3

The government and the corporate giants are both the product of the depression and recession of the recent years. Most of the income we made went into paying taxes and interests to financial institutions and the government.

In 2006, in the most populated state, one would not be able to find a decent single family home with three bedrooms, two baths, and in a good school district for under $300,000. Consequently, around that same year, the government has raised its conforming loan limits to $417,000 from $359,000 for single-family homes.

The reported and unreported income of Americans was overlooked in the consideration of affordability of a $300,000 loan. Current income data published by the Census Bureau was overlooked and ignored This data showed that current household income of most Americans, even with no income verification, could not afford these homes.

Technically speaking, the real estate boom (as it was projected) was a tidal wave. In the spirit of not wanting to be left behind, you sail your boat on it and ride with all that you have. When you consider a median income of $43,000 to purchase or refinance a home for $300,000, in a good school district for your kids because their education is important to you. An FHA loan would allow about 31% of that income for your mortgage, which will make it impossible for most of us to purchase a home in this market.

If you approach the market with what you can afford, as show in figure 4, a conventional loan program with the government (like Fannie Mae and Freddie Mac) would allow you to use 28% and 31% of your income, consecutively, toward your mortgage payment. The sub-prime and nonconforming world would limit you at 55%. Consecutively, $13,000of your income is used with an FHA loan for a PITI of $1083, $12,000 with a conventional loan for a PITI of $1,000, and about $24,000 with nonconforming loan for a PITI of $2000.

Remember, your debt-to-income ratio for your mortgage payment is a combination of principal, interest, taxes, and insurance (also known at PITI). In the market, this $300,000 loan would yield a PITI of $2,594 per month with an FHA program of 6% interest rate, a PITI of $2,691 per month for conventional loan with a 6.5% interest rate, and a PITI of $2,893 for a nonconforming loan with a 7% interest rate.

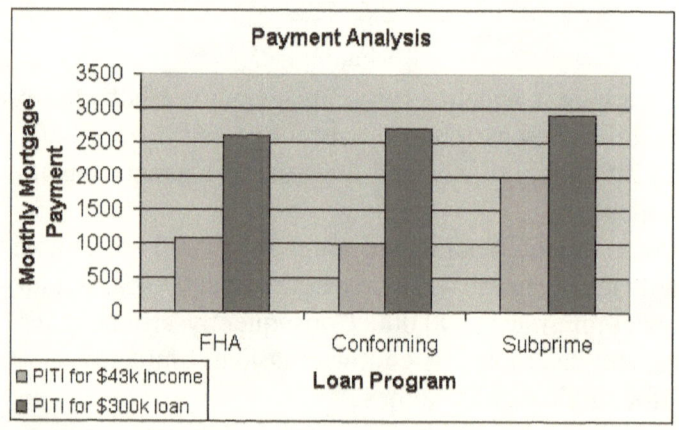

One would need an annual income of over $100,000 to afford a house in 2006, whether it be an FHA, conventional, or nonconforming loan. In fact, most homes in the past few years were financed with nonconforming loans as more people were unable to verify their income (or incomes) and could not support these purchases. Government and the lenders know very well that you could no longer afford these homes because their data reveals that clearly. Again, about *90% of Americans* make less than $100,000 per year. It was impossible for *us,* the *people,* to survive this market.

The banking institution and many investment portfolios with large capital in the market wanted this tidal wave to keep going at any costs. These institutions were also appalled by the idea of putting *us,* the *people,* in homes we cannot even afford. Theoretically speaking, the trends showed home prices would continue to double. People just did not have the means to support these expenditures that came with home-price inflation. Simply, there is no way to sustain a family when over 70% of your income is consumed by a mortgage payment over a long period. We are then left with 25% for other obligations. By the way, this is assuming we don't pay any Federal taxes, 7.5% of income goes toward social security and Medicare taxes.

So we are actually left with 17% for everything else like autos, food, education, day care, health insurance, utilities, etc. No amount of overtime, benefits, and bonuses could save us from a titanic disaster. Most payment delinquencies were a product of job loss, coupled with pay cuts, as the economy began to weaken.

Many institutions that were looking for large gains after the crash of the stock market in early 2000 turned to real estate to rescue them from the stock market financial disaster. The so-called experts began to make a case for our money in these real estate investments (derivatives), and now we are being told they acted with bad intelligence. *They got bushed*, so they say. These people are the real *flip-floppers*. Profits seemed to baffle the mind of the intellect and their judgments are, at best, that of an infant, excited to play with his or her toy and unaware of any possible side effects.

We are constantly told the only way to create wealth is to reinvest our savings to compensate for inflation. Really, this is a neat idea, but where are they putting this money? Do not tell them I told you that. Our income is not really in our control, and those who want to control it cannot since we lost most of the value of our investment to the real estate and stock market in less than a decade. If you don't know, most banks use about 90¢ of every dollar you deposit right away to cover their withdrawals, losses, and the large returns they promised to you, as well as a host of other things. So your money is always at risk even when it is insured by the Federal Deposit Insurance Corporation (FDIC).

Our income is what everyone has an eye on. Money managers invest our money into high net worth investments despite evidence of market volatility. There are times one will realize consistent, steady gains and times gradual losses are realized. Often losses produce shock waves to investors everywhere, as though it was always unexpected. Real Estate investment was one sure investment everyone relied on to put his or her money into. However, they failed to tell you, what goes up must come down. Someone would eventually lose. In most cases, we the people lose because it is the consumers that consume these products. I do not think we can avoid losses, but we can minimize these losses.

We should never gamble again with the real estate market, as we now know everything ties to it. In fact, the real estate market is the second

15

largest component of the gross domestic product (GDP) at 10% (health care being the first at 12%).

We will depend on our income for many years to come. In fact, people are living beyond seventy-five years old these days. Our existence depends on our ability to support ourselves. So decisions made about our income could have an eventual dire consequence in our lives.

Chapter 2

Debts

These days, you cannot turn on the radio or the television without hearing a conversation about the debt crisis of this nation. In fact, financial gurus are telling you to pay down, or pay off, your debts. Some debts are good, and others are bad. You see, for some time you were being told the only way to build your credit is by having a few credit cards (also known as revolving debts). You were told you must make use of these credit cards, and they must not remain idle in order to improve your credit score.

In fact, some creditors automatically increase credit limits for excellent payment history and maintaining a reasonable balance. Ironically, creditors spur spending by raising credit limits of good-payment-history clients. This increase of access to credit is naturally tempting and the foundation of mismanaged credit. Credit card companies make it flexible with just a small monthly payment. You then become less restless about the balance of your credit cards with these suitable monthly payments. In fact, the premise of credit cards is to retain the balance in your credit card; therefore, payment structure is formulated to ensure a nearly infinite annuity period. This produces an endless accumulation of interest for the creditors. This is why credit card issuers find it logical to influence the credit user's purchasing habits through credit limit increases, thus making it harder to pay off credit balances. Creditors intentionally want credit card balances to be unbearable to make certain you spend the rest of your life paying credit card bills.

As I was doing my research for this book, I was in disbelief with some of the things I read. Mathematics is great a science and its application can be both plausible and implausible. Credit is a form of debt financing. A few mathematical formulas and strategies are employed to manage these investment vehicles.

Banks used to compound interest *quarterly*. That meant that four times a year they would have an "interest day," when everybody's balance got bumped up by one fourth of the going interest rate . . . and bank employees would have to work late, going home all sweaty and covered with ink. If you held an account in those days, every year your balance would increase by a factor of $(1 + r/4)4$ where r is the rate. Today it's possible to compound interest monthly, daily, and in the limiting case, *continuously*, meaning that your balance grows by a small amount every instant.

Clearly, something has to change if we are to survive this recurring theme of economic hardship. Most credit card companies compound their interest daily; this should be outlawed. I do not think we will ever see an investment for the *people* that will receive a risk free daily dose of compounding interest. We also do not expect this to happen either; we just want to keep more of our money so we can do the things we need to do. Creditors cannot be happy when your balance is zero. You then remain their target with exciting introductory purchase interest rate.

The example below shows using compound interest assuming a perfect world—your money can grow very quickly without doing anything at all. What they may not tell you is they turn around and take that same money to sell and buy securities in the form of a mortgage, or a car loan to you and me. The compounding interest formula may be magical, but the mortgage formula is overloaded (excessive), thus overshadowing the magic of the compounding interest.

Example

Compound Interest (Future Value)

Suppose you open an account that pays a guaranteed interest rate, compounded annually. You make no further contributions; you just leave your money alone and let compound interest work its magic.

The balance your account has grown at some point in the future is known as the *future value* of your starting principal.

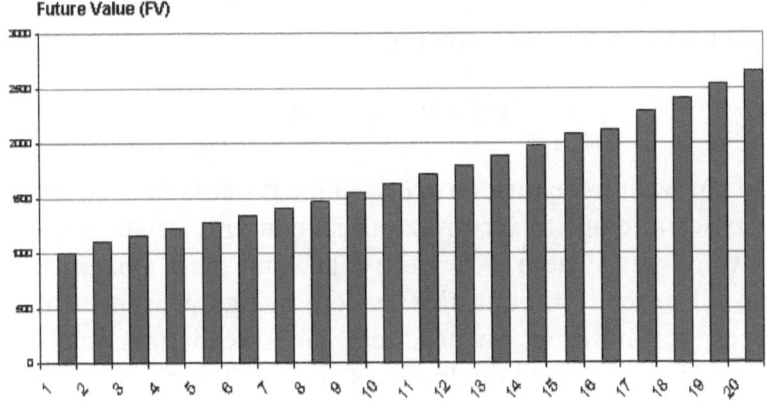

Future Value (FV)

To find a formula for future value, we will write P for your starting principal, and r for the rate of return expressed as a decimal. (So if the interest rate is 5%, r equals .05). Your balance will grow according to the following schedule:

Year	Balance
Now	P
1	$P + rP$
2	$(P + rP) + r(P + rP)$

This starts to get messy in a hurry. But you can simplify it by noticing that you can keep pulling out factors of $(1 + r)$ from each line. If you do that, the balances collapse to a simple pattern:

Year	Balance
Now	P
1	$P(1 + r)$
2	$P(1 + r)^2$

If you follow this pattern out for Y years, you get the general formula for future value:

1. $$FV = P (1 + r)^Y$$

19

That is to compound once per year. More generally, if you want to compound n times per year, you use:

$$FV = P \left(1 + r/n\right)^{Yn}$$

I do not want to be misconstrued in the process of shedding some lights as we attempt to scrutinize this economic crisis and explore the flaws of our system. After all, that very same system fails us. We can all agree, although this system brings prosperity in some instances, its malfunction produces massive depression, dearth, heartache, famine, and hopelessness. Just as the country functions much better when it governs from the middle, this economy will also thrive by restoring a sense of balance in the system. We can start with mortgage finance.

Mortgage

You can think of a mortgage as either building up equity or paying off debt. Although the payments are all equal, equity does not build up at a constant rate: that's because at the beginning, the debt is still high, so most of the payments are paying interest; toward the end, the remaining debt is small, so very little of the payment goes toward interest.

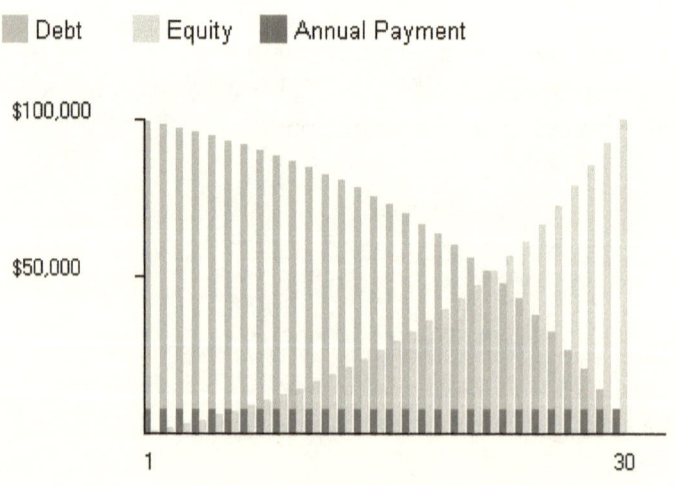

If you look at what's happening to the debt, you'll see it's similar to an annuity; only now, you're paying the balance off rather than using it up. Also, the timing is slightly different: you make your first payment at the *end* of the first year.

Let's write a formula for the annual payment amount, and write z for (1 + r); P is the initial loan amount, and r is the loan interest rate expressed as a decimal. Writing out the remaining debt at the end of the first few years,

Year	Debt
1	$Pz - a$
2	$(Pz - a)z - a$
3	$[(Pz - a)z - a]z - a$

Multiplying the right sides yields the pattern:

Year	Debt
1	$Pz - a$
2	$Pz^2 - az - a$
3	$Pz^3 - az^2 - az - a$
Y	$Pz^Y - a(1 + z + z^2 + \ldots + z^{Y-1})$

The second part of the last line is a times the sum of a geometric series. So the formula simplifies to:

$$\text{Debt}(Y) = Pz^Y - a[(z^Y - 1)/(z - 1)]$$

We're assuming that P, r, and Y are all known and that we want to find a that makes the debt balance go to zero at time Y; so set $\text{Debt}(Y) = 0$ and solve for a, to get:

$$0 = Pz^Y - a[(z^Y - 1)/(z - 1)]$$
$$a = [Pz^Y]/[(z^Y - 1)/(z - 1)]$$
$$a = [Pz^Y(z - 1)]/[z^Y - 1]$$

Finally, write z out in terms of r, to get the mortgage formula:

$$a = [\, P(1 + r)^Y r \,] / [\, (1 + r)^Y - 1]$$

Example

Suppose you take out a thirty-year mortgage for $100,000 at 7% interest and want to know the monthly payments. To do that, you divide the interest rate by 12 to get (.07/12) = .00583; and multiply 30 x 12 = 360 to get the number of payments. Then the formula gives you:

payment = [$100,000(1 + .00583)^{360} x .00583] / [(1 + .00583)^{360} - 1] = $665

My theory is all debts are bad. We need to learn to live within our means. We create current debts to be paid by future profits. Well, if this profit never comes, we are in this for the long run. When you take on a debt your income cannot afford, you only put yourself in even deeper debt. These debts will use up all the savings. This is where, if you don't manage already scarce income, we will never be able to retire with the current disproportional system.

In the following example, I am going to show the impact debts can have on a family of three with a mortgage, two credit cards, small savings, and a yearly income of $84,995.

Typical American Family Expense

Total Projected Cost	% of income
$8,464	119%

Projected Monthly Income	
Income 1	$4,249.58
Income 2	$2,854.17
Extra income	
Total monthly income	$7,104

Housing	Projected Cost	% of income
Mortgage (PITI) or rent	$2,699	38.00%
Transportation	$1,350	19.00%
Food Budget	$995	14.00%
Alcohol	$142	2.00%
Tobacco and related products	$213	3.00%
caffeine related products	$142	2.00%
Clothing & related services	$355	5.00%
Life insurance	$71	1.00%
Out of Pocket Health care	$426	6.00%
Investments	$355	5.00%
Entertainment	$355	5.00%
Charitable contributions	$178	2.50%
Beauty products	$71	1.00%
Miscellaneous	$142	2.00%
credit cards	$284	4.00%
Social security	$440	6.20%
Maintenance	$103	1.45%
Reading & Education	$142	2.00%
Totals	$8,464	119.15%

At first glance, the above table showed that the American family exceeded their *monthly* budget by almost 20%. These numbers are already astounding without even factoring in federal, state, and local taxes into the equation. Most analysts will tell you to cut down on your expenses. While this is very true, I do not think you need any more of this failed lecture. Here is what I observe: Despite the drastic price reduction in home values, most current homebuyers may want to sell their homes in seven years time, most likely because of job relocation, would be faced with the grim fact (or the surprise) that these homes have barely appreciated and, most likely have devalued. You will have spent an amount of $226,716 toward your home. This is an equivalent of 2.67 years of income. At this point, you will have only paid 10% toward the principal. Given the current inventory, properties are not expected to gain much value for several years to come. So long term really means you cannot move or relocate—you are stuck until you build equity (the house appreciates).

If we are going to be lectured about living above our means, we are willing to listen and make some cuts, but we soon become disheartened as we begin to see how the pendulum always swings the way of the lending institutions. If the government and banking institutions are not willing to change the system to remedy the situation, we will find ourselves in a negative amortization situation after a few years. The only way to avoid this increase is to put more money down on your home or pay cash for it. This will drastically reduce the final amount of money this home will cost. Even then, one has to be very careful understanding any capital invested in this current real estate market without a long-term plan of 20 years, the risk is high.

The absence of the aforementioned preconceived notion in the mind of the homebuyers can exacerbate the potential real estate market recovery. Homebuyers beware if your plan is to get rich quick. This market is not for you. On the other hand if you want to get wealthy, then maybe you should invest and understand the long term wealth recovery period that comes with this uncertain market future.

Chapter 3

Amortization Schedule

The current amortization schedule used by lending institutions around the world offers a front-load interest mechanism that appropriately returns the capital invested by these institutions in the early years of the mortgage loan. This chapter will closely analyze the impact of the current amortization schedule, which requires extraordinary changes in these extraordinary times.

Assume a family of three takes out a mortgage loan for $100,000 in a house they recently purchase. This property may not have been a huge house, but enough to keep the family safe in today's market. The credit rating of this family is fair and able to get a 6% interest rate. The amortization schedule displayed below yields the following benefit to this family and lending institution.

The lending institution will recuperate the money they invested in about twenty years, or 248 payments (see payment number 248 in table below), and assuming the interest rate as a percentage of principal is 115% over a thirty-year period. The monthly principal and interest (PI) payment would be $599.55, and the homeowner would have paid down its principal loan balance by 48% after these 248 payments. Considering the homeowner taxes are about $891 a year and homeowner insurance is about $1,750 per year, the principal, interest, taxes, and insurance (PITI) would be $819.63 per month (less mortgage premium insurance). The Federal Housing Administration (FHA) loan program would require at least a household income of about $29,000 to qualify for this mortgage.

Pmt	Principal	Interest	Cum Prin	Cum Int	Prin Bal
1	99.55	500.00	99.55	500.00	99900.45
2	100.05	499.50	199.60	999.50	99800.40
3	100.55	499.00	300.15	1498.50	99699.85
4	101.05	498.50	401.20	1997.00	99598.80
5	101.56	497.99	502.76	2494.99	99497.24
6	102.06	497.49	604.82	2992.48	99395.18
7	102.57	496.98	707.39	3489.46	99292.61
8	103.09	496.46	810.48	3985.92	99189.52
9	103.60	495.95	914.08	4481.87	99085.92
10	104.12	495.43	1018.20	4977.30	98981.80
11	104.64	494.91	1122.84	5472.21	98877.16
12	105.16	494.39	1228.00	5966.60	98772.00
13	105.69	493.86	1333.69	6460.46	98666.31
14	106.22	493.33	1439.91	6953.79	98560.09
15	106.75	492.80	1546.66	7446.59	98453.34
16	107.28	492.27	1653.94	7938.86	98346.06
17	107.82	491.73	1761.76	8430.59	98238.24
18	108.36	491.19	1870.12	8921.78	98129.88
19	108.90	490.65	1979.02	9412.43	98020.98
20	109.45	490.10	2088.47	9902.53	97911.53
21	109.99	489.56	2198.46	10392.09	97801.54
22	110.54	489.01	2309.00	10881.10	97691.00
23	111.10	488.45	2420.10	11369.55	97579.90
24	111.65	487.90	2531.75	11857.45	97468.25
25	112.21	487.34	2643.96	12344.79	97356.04
26	112.77	486.78	2756.73	12831.57	97243.27
27	113.33	486.22	2870.06	13317.79	97129.94
28	113.90	485.65	2983.96	13803.44	97016.04
29	114.47	485.08	3098.43	14288.52	96901.57

Pmt	Principal	Interest	Cum Prin	Cum Int	Prin Bal
30	115.04	484.51	3213.47	14773.03	96786.53
31	115.62	483.93	3329.09	15256.96	96670.91
32	116.20	483.35	3445.29	15740.31	96554.71
33	116.78	482.77	3562.07	16223.08	96437.93
34	117.36	482.19	3679.43	16705.27	96320.57
35	117.95	481.60	3797.38	17186.87	96202.62
36	118.54	481.01	3915.92	17667.88	96084.08
37	119.13	480.42	4035.05	18148.30	95964.95
38	119.73	479.82	4154.78	18628.12	95845.22
39	120.32	479.23	4275.10	19107.35	95724.90
40	120.93	478.62	4396.03	19585.97	95603.97
41	121.53	478.02	4517.56	20063.99	95482.44
42	122.14	477.41	4639.70	20541.40	95360.30
43	122.75	476.80	4762.45	21018.20	95237.55
44	123.36	476.19	4885.81	21494.39	95114.19
45	123.98	475.57	5009.79	21969.96	94990.21
46	124.60	474.95	5134.39	22444.91	94865.61
47	125.22	474.33	5259.61	22919.24	94740.39
48	125.85	473.70	5385.46	23392.94	94614.54
49	126.48	473.07	5511.94	23866.01	94488.06
50	127.11	472.44	5639.05	24338.45	94360.95
51	127.75	471.80	5766.80	24810.25	94233.20
52	128.38	471.17	5895.18	25281.42	94104.82
53	129.03	470.52	6024.21	25751.94	93975.79
54	129.67	469.88	6153.88	26221.82	93846.12
55	130.32	469.23	6284.20	26691.05	93715.80
56	130.97	468.58	6415.17	27159.63	93584.83
57	131.63	467.92	6546.80	27627.55	93453.20

Pmt	Principal	Interest	Cum Prin	Cum Int	Prin Bal
58	132.28	467.27	6679.08	28094.82	93320.92
59	132.95	466.60	6812.03	28561.42	93187.97
60	133.61	465.94	6945.64	29027.36	93054.36
61	134.28	465.27	7079.92	29492.63	92920.08
62	134.95	464.60	7214.87	29957.23	92785.13
63	135.62	463.93	7350.49	30421.16	92649.51
64	136.30	463.25	7486.79	30884.41	92513.21
65	136.98	462.57	7623.77	31346.98	92376.23
66	137.67	461.88	7761.44	31808.86	92238.56
67	138.36	461.19	7899.80	32270.05	92100.20
68	139.05	460.50	8038.85	32730.55	91961.15
69	139.74	459.81	8178.59	33190.36	91821.41
70	140.44	459.11	8319.03	33649.47	91680.97
71	141.15	458.40	8460.18	34107.87	91539.82
72	141.85	457.70	8602.03	34565.57	91397.97
73	142.56	456.99	8744.59	35022.56	91255.41
74	143.27	456.28	8887.86	35478.84	91112.14
75	143.99	455.56	9031.85	35934.40	90968.15
76	144.71	454.84	9176.56	36389.24	90823.44
77	145.43	454.12	9321.99	36843.36	90678.01
78	146.16	453.39	9468.15	37296.75	90531.85
79	146.89	452.66	9615.04	37749.41	90384.96
80	147.63	451.92	9762.67	38201.33	90237.33
81	148.36	451.19	9911.03	38652.52	90088.97
82	149.11	450.44	10060.14	39102.96	89939.86
83	149.85	449.70	10209.99	39552.66	89790.01
84	150.60	448.95	10360.59	40001.61	89639.41
85	151.35	448.20	10511.94	40449.81	89488.06

Pmt	Principal	Interest	Cum Prin	Cum Int	Prin Bal
86	152.11	447.44	10664.05	40897.25	89335.95
87	152.87	446.68	10816.92	41343.93	89183.08
88	153.63	445.92	10970.55	41789.85	89029.45
89	154.40	445.15	11124.95	42235.00	88875.05
90	155.17	444.38	11280.12	42679.38	88719.88
91	155.95	443.60	11436.07	43122.98	88563.93
92	156.73	442.82	11592.80	43565.80	88407.20
93	157.51	442.04	11750.31	44007.84	88249.69
94	158.30	441.25	11908.61	44449.09	88091.39
95	159.09	440.46	12067.70	44889.55	87932.30
96	159.89	439.66	12227.59	45329.21	87772.41
97	160.69	438.86	12388.28	45768.07	87611.72
98	161.49	438.06	12549.77	46206.13	87450.23
99	162.30	437.25	12712.07	46643.38	87287.93
100	163.11	436.44	12875.18	47079.82	87124.82
101	163.93	435.62	13039.11	47515.44	86960.89
102	164.75	434.80	13203.86	47950.24	86796.14
103	165.57	433.98	13369.43	48384.22	86630.57
104	166.40	433.15	13535.83	48817.37	86464.17
105	167.23	432.32	13703.06	49249.69	86296.94
106	168.07	431.48	13871.13	49681.17	86128.87
107	168.91	430.64	14040.04	50111.81	85959.96
108	169.75	429.80	14209.79	50541.61	85790.21
109	170.60	428.95	14380.39	50970.56	85619.61
110	171.45	428.10	14551.84	51398.66	85448.16
111	172.31	427.24	14724.15	51825.90	85275.85
112	173.17	426.38	14897.32	52252.28	85102.68
113	174.04	425.51	15071.36	52677.79	84928.64

Pmt	Principal	Interest	Cum Prin	Cum Int	Prin Bal
114	174.91	424.64	15246.27	53102.43	84753.73
115	175.78	423.77	15422.05	53526.20	84577.95
116	176.66	422.89	15598.71	53949.09	84401.29
117	177.54	422.01	15776.25	54371.10	84223.75
118	178.43	421.12	15954.68	54792.22	84045.32
119	179.32	420.23	16134.00	55212.45	83866.00
120	180.22	419.33	16314.22	55631.78	83685.78
121	181.12	418.43	16495.34	56050.21	83504.66
122	182.03	417.52	16677.37	56467.73	83322.63
123	182.94	416.61	16860.31	56884.34	83139.69
124	183.85	415.70	17044.16	57300.04	82955.84
125	184.77	414.78	17228.93	57714.82	82771.07
126	185.69	413.86	17414.62	58128.68	82585.38
127	186.62	412.93	17601.24	58541.61	82398.76
128	187.56	411.99	17788.80	58953.60	82211.20
129	188.49	411.06	17977.29	59364.66	82022.71
130	189.44	410.11	18166.73	59774.77	81833.27
131	190.38	409.17	18357.11	60183.94	81642.89
132	191.34	408.21	18548.45	60592.15	81451.55
133	192.29	407.26	18740.74	60999.41	81259.26
134	193.25	406.30	18933.99	61405.71	81066.01
135	194.22	405.33	19128.21	61811.04	80871.79
136	195.19	404.36	19323.40	62215.40	80676.60
137	196.17	403.38	19519.57	62618.78	80480.43
138	197.15	402.40	19716.72	63021.18	80283.28
139	198.13	401.42	19914.85	63422.60	80085.15
140	199.12	400.43	20113.97	63823.03	79886.03
141	200.12	399.43	20314.09	64222.46	79685.91
142	201.12	398.43	20515.21	64620.89	79484.79

Pmt	Principal	Interest	Cum Prin	Cum Int	Prin Bal
143	202.13	397.42	20717.34	65018.31	79282.66
144	203.14	396.41	20920.48	65414.72	79079.52
145	204.15	395.40	21124.63	65810.12	78875.37
146	205.17	394.38	21329.80	66204.50	78670.20
147	206.20	393.35	21536.00	66597.85	78464.00
148	207.23	392.32	21743.23	66990.17	78256.77
149	208.27	391.28	21951.50	67381.45	78048.50
150	209.31	390.24	22160.81	67771.69	77839.19
151	210.35	389.20	22371.16	68160.89	77628.84
152	211.41	388.14	22582.57	68549.03	77417.43
153	212.46	387.09	22795.03	68936.12	77204.97
154	213.53	386.02	23008.56	69322.14	76991.44
155	214.59	384.96	23223.15	69707.10	76776.85
156	215.67	383.88	23438.82	70090.98	76561.18
157	216.74	382.81	23655.56	70473.79	76344.44
158	217.83	381.72	23873.39	70855.51	76126.61
159	218.92	380.63	24092.31	71236.14	75907.69
160	220.01	379.54	24312.32	71615.68	75687.68
161	221.11	378.44	24533.43	71994.12	75466.57
162	222.22	377.33	24755.65	72371.45	75244.35
163	223.33	376.22	24978.98	72747.67	75021.02
164	224.44	375.11	25203.42	73122.78	74796.58
165	225.57	373.98	25428.99	73496.76	74571.01
166	226.69	372.86	25655.68	73869.62	74344.32
167	227.83	371.72	25883.51	74241.34	74116.49
168	228.97	370.58	26112.48	74611.92	73887.52
169	230.11	369.44	26342.59	74981.36	73657.41

Pmt	Principal	Interest	Cum Prin	Cum Int	Prin Bal
170	231.26	368.29	26573.85	75349.65	73426.15
171	232.42	367.13	26806.27	75716.78	73193.73
172	233.58	365.97	27039.85	76082.75	72960.15
173	234.75	364.80	27274.60	76447.55	72725.40
174	235.92	363.63	27510.52	76811.18	72489.48
175	237.10	362.45	27747.62	77173.63	72252.38
176	238.29	361.26	27985.91	77534.89	72014.09
177	239.48	360.07	28225.39	77894.96	71774.61
178	240.68	358.87	28466.07	78253.83	71533.93
179	241.88	357.67	28707.95	78611.50	71292.05
180	243.09	356.46	28951.04	78967.96	71048.96
181	244.31	355.24	29195.35	79323.20	70804.65
182	245.53	354.02	29440.88	79677.22	70559.12
183	246.75	352.80	29687.63	80030.02	70312.37
184	247.99	351.56	29935.62	80381.58	70064.38
185	249.23	350.32	30184.85	80731.90	69815.15
186	250.47	349.08	30435.32	81080.98	69564.68
187	251.73	347.82	30687.05	81428.80	69312.95
188	252.99	346.56	30940.04	81775.36	69059.96
189	254.25	345.30	31194.29	82120.66	68805.71
190	255.52	344.03	31449.81	82464.69	68550.19
191	256.80	342.75	31706.61	82807.44	68293.39
192	258.08	341.47	31964.69	83148.91	68035.31
193	259.37	340.18	32224.06	83489.09	67775.94
194	260.67	338.88	32484.73	83827.97	67515.27
195	261.97	337.58	32746.70	84165.55	67253.30
196	263.28	336.27	33009.98	84501.82	66990.02
197	264.60	334.95	33274.58	84836.77	66725.42

Pmt	Principal	Interest	Cum Prin	Cum Int	Prin Bal
198	265.92	333.63	33540.50	85170.40	66459.50
199	267.25	332.30	33807.75	85502.70	66192.25
200	268.59	330.96	34076.34	85833.66	65923.66
201	269.93	329.62	34346.27	86163.28	65653.73
202	271.28	328.27	34617.55	86491.55	65382.45
203	272.64	326.91	34890.19	86818.46	65109.81
204	274.00	325.55	35164.19	87144.01	64835.81
205	275.37	324.18	35439.56	87468.19	64560.44
206	276.75	322.80	35716.31	87790.99	64283.69
207	278.13	321.42	35994.44	88112.41	64005.56
208	279.52	320.03	36273.96	88432.44	63726.04
209	280.92	318.63	36554.88	88751.07	63445.12
210	282.32	317.23	36837.20	89068.30	63162.80
211	283.74	315.81	37120.94	89384.11	62879.06
212	285.15	314.40	37406.09	89698.51	62593.91
213	286.58	312.97	37692.67	90011.48	62307.33
214	288.01	311.54	37980.68	90323.02	62019.32
215	289.45	310.10	38270.13	90633.12	61729.87
216	290.90	308.65	38561.03	90941.77	61438.97
217	292.36	307.19	38853.39	91248.96	61146.61
218	293.82	305.73	39147.21	91554.69	60852.79
219	295.29	304.26	39442.50	91858.95	60557.50
220	296.76	302.79	39739.26	92161.74	60260.74
221	298.25	301.30	40037.51	92463.04	59962.49
222	299.74	299.81	40337.25	92762.85	59662.75
223	301.24	298.31	40638.49	93061.16	59361.51
224	302.74	296.81	40941.23	93357.97	59058.77
225	304.26	295.29	41245.49	93653.26	58754.51
226	305.78	293.77	41551.27	93947.03	58448.73

Pmt	Principal	Interest	Cum Prin	Cum Int	Prin Bal
227	307.31	292.24	41858.58	94239.27	58141.42
228	308.84	290.71	42167.42	94529.98	57832.58
229	310.39	289.16	42477.81	94819.14	57522.19
230	311.94	287.61	42789.75	95106.75	57210.25
231	313.50	286.05	43103.25	95392.80	56896.75
232	315.07	284.48	43418.32	95677.28	56581.68
233	316.64	282.91	43734.96	95960.19	56265.04
234	318.22	281.33	44053.18	96241.52	55946.82
235	319.82	279.73	44373.00	96521.25	55627.00
236	321.42	278.13	44694.42	96799.38	55305.58
237	323.02	276.53	45017.44	97075.91	54982.56
238	324.64	274.91	45342.08	97350.82	54657.92
239	326.26	273.29	45668.34	97624.11	54331.66
240	327.89	271.66	45996.23	97895.77	54003.77
241	329.53	270.02	46325.76	98165.79	53674.24
242	331.18	268.37	46656.94	98434.16	53343.06
243	332.83	266.72	46989.77	98700.88	53010.23
244	334.50	265.05	47324.27	98965.93	52675.73
245	336.17	263.38	47660.44	99229.31	52339.56
246	337.85	261.70	47998.29	99491.01	52001.71
247	339.54	260.01	48337.83	99751.02	51662.17
248	341.24	258.31	**48679.07**	**100009.33**	51320.93
249	342.95	256.60	49022.02	100265.93	50977.98
250	344.66	254.89	49366.68	100520.82	50633.32
251	346.38	253.17	49713.06	100773.99	50286.94
252	348.12	251.43	50061.18	101025.42	49938.82
253	349.86	249.69	50411.04	101275.11	49588.96

Pmt	Principal	Interest	Cum Prin	Cum Int	Prin Bal
254	351.61	247.94	50762.65	101523.05	49237.35
255	353.36	246.19	51116.01	101769.24	48883.99
256	355.13	244.42	51471.14	102013.66	48528.86
257	356.91	242.64	51828.05	102256.30	48171.95
258	358.69	240.86	52186.74	102497.16	47813.26
259	360.48	239.07	52547.22	102736.23	47452.78
260	362.29	237.26	52909.51	102973.49	47090.49
261	364.10	235.45	53273.61	103208.94	46726.39
262	365.92	233.63	53639.53	103442.57	46360.47
263	367.75	231.80	54007.28	103674.37	45992.72
264	369.59	229.96	54376.87	103904.33	45623.13
265	371.43	228.12	54748.30	104132.45	45251.70
266	373.29	226.26	55121.59	104358.71	44878.41
267	375.16	224.39	55496.75	104583.10	44503.25
268	377.03	222.52	55873.78	104805.62	44126.22
269	378.92	220.63	56252.70	105026.25	43747.30
270	380.81	218.74	56633.51	105244.99	43366.49
271	382.72	216.83	57016.23	105461.82	42983.77
272	384.63	214.92	57400.86	105676.74	42599.14
273	386.55	213.00	57787.41	105889.74	42212.59
274	388.49	211.06	58175.90	106100.80	41824.10
275	390.43	209.12	58566.33	106309.92	41433.67
276	392.38	207.17	58958.71	106517.09	41041.29
277	394.34	205.21	59353.05	106722.30	40646.95
278	396.32	203.23	59749.37	106925.53	40250.63
279	398.30	201.25	60147.67	107126.78	39852.33
280	400.29	199.26	60547.96	107326.04	39452.04
281	402.29	197.26	60950.25	107523.30	39049.75

Pmt	Principal	Interest	Cum Prin	Cum Int	Prin Bal
282	404.30	195.25	61354.55	107718.55	38645.45
283	406.32	193.23	61760.87	107911.78	38239.13
284	408.35	191.20	62169.22	108102.98	37830.78
285	410.40	189.15	62579.62	108292.13	37420.38
286	412.45	187.10	62992.07	108479.23	37007.93
287	414.51	185.04	63406.58	108664.27	36593.42
288	416.58	182.97	63823.16	108847.24	36176.84
289	418.67	180.88	64241.83	109028.12	35758.17
290	420.76	178.79	64662.59	109206.91	35337.41
291	422.86	176.69	65085.45	109383.60	34914.55
292	424.98	174.57	65510.43	109558.17	34489.57
293	427.10	172.45	65937.53	109730.62	34062.47
294	429.24	170.31	66366.77	109900.93	33633.23
295	431.38	168.17	66798.15	110069.10	33201.85
296	433.54	166.01	67231.69	110235.11	32768.31
297	435.71	163.84	67667.40	110398.95	32332.60
298	437.89	161.66	68105.29	110560.61	31894.71
299	440.08	159.47	68545.37	110720.08	31454.63
300	442.28	157.27	68987.65	110877.35	31012.35
301	444.49	155.06	69432.14	111032.41	30567.86
302	446.71	152.84	69878.85	111185.25	30121.15
303	448.94	150.61	70327.79	111335.86	29672.21
304	451.19	148.36	70778.98	111484.22	29221.02
305	453.44	146.11	71232.42	111630.33	28767.58
306	455.71	143.84	71688.13	111774.17	28311.87
307	457.99	141.56	72146.12	111915.73	27853.88
308	460.28	139.27	72606.40	112055.00	27393.60
309	462.58	136.97	73068.98	112191.97	26931.02
310	464.89	134.66	73533.87	112326.63	26466.13

Pmt	Principal	Interest	Cum Prin	Cum Int	Prin Bal
311	467.22	132.33	74001.09	112458.96	25998.91
312	469.56	129.99	74470.65	112588.95	25529.35
313	471.90	127.65	74942.55	112716.60	25057.45
314	474.26	125.29	75416.81	112841.89	24583.19
315	476.63	122.92	75893.44	112964.81	24106.56
316	479.02	120.53	76372.46	113085.34	23627.54
317	481.41	118.14	76853.87	113203.48	23146.13
318	483.82	115.73	77337.69	113319.21	22662.31
319	486.24	113.31	77823.93	113432.52	22176.07
320	488.67	110.88	78312.60	113543.40	21687.40
321	491.11	108.44	78803.71	113651.84	21196.29
322	493.57	105.98	79297.28	113757.82	20702.72
323	496.04	103.51	79793.32	113861.33	20206.68
324	498.52	101.03	80291.84	113962.36	19708.16
325	501.01	98.54	80792.85	114060.90	19207.15
326	503.51	96.04	81296.36	114156.94	18703.64
327	506.03	93.52	81802.39	114250.46	18197.61
328	508.56	90.99	82310.95	114341.45	17689.05
329	511.10	88.45	82822.05	114429.90	17177.95
330	513.66	85.89	83335.71	114515.79	16664.29
331	516.23	83.32	83851.94	114599.11	16148.06
332	518.81	80.74	84370.75	114679.85	15629.25
333	521.40	78.15	84892.15	114758.00	15107.85
334	524.01	75.54	85416.16	114833.54	14583.84
335	526.63	72.92	85942.79	114906.46	14057.21
336	529.26	70.29	86472.05	114976.75	13527.95
337	531.91	67.64	87003.96	115044.39	12996.04

Pmt	Principal	Interest	Cum Prin	Cum Int	Prin Bal
338	534.57	64.98	87538.53	115109.37	12461.47
339	537.24	62.31	88075.77	115171.68	11924.23
340	539.93	59.62	88615.70	115231.30	11384.30
341	542.63	56.92	89158.33	115288.22	10841.67
342	545.34	54.21	89703.67	115342.43	10296.33
343	548.07	51.48	90251.74	115393.91	9748.26
344	550.81	48.74	90802.55	115442.65	9197.45
345	553.56	45.99	91356.11	115488.64	8643.89
346	556.33	43.22	91912.44	115531.86	8087.56
347	559.11	40.44	92471.55	115572.30	7528.45
348	561.91	37.64	93033.46	115609.94	6966.54
349	564.72	34.83	93598.18	115644.77	6401.82
350	567.54	32.01	94165.72	115676.78	5834.28
351	570.38	29.17	94736.10	115705.95	5263.90
352	573.23	26.32	95309.33	115732.27	4690.67
353	576.10	23.45	95885.43	115755.72	4114.57
354	578.98	20.57	96464.41	115776.29	3535.59
355	581.87	17.68	97046.28	115793.97	2953.72
356	584.78	14.77	97631.06	115808.74	2368.94
357	587.71	11.84	98218.77	115820.58	1781.23
358	590.64	8.91	98809.41	115829.49	1190.59
359	593.60	5.95	99403.01	115835.44	596.99
360	596.57	2.98	99999.58	115838.42	0.42

If the interest rate was at 7%, figure 4 showed that the lending institution would recuperate their investment in sixteen years or roughly 195 payments of $665.30(PI); however, the homeowner would have paid down 29% of the principal loan balance. This yields a PITI payment of $885.38 per month. The interest as percentage of principal is 140%. An average household income of $32,000 is required to qualify for this loan.

Pmt	Principal	Interest	Cum Prin	Cum Int	Prin Bal
1	81.97	583.33	81.97	583.33	99918.03
2	82.44	582.86	164.41	1166.19	99835.59
3	82.93	582.37	247.34	1748.56	99752.66
4	83.41	581.89	330.75	2330.45	99669.25
5	83.90	581.40	414.65	2911.85	99585.35
6	84.39	580.91	499.04	3492.76	99500.96
7	84.88	580.42	583.92	4073.18	99416.08
8	85.37	579.93	669.29	4653.11	99330.71
9	85.87	579.43	755.16	5232.54	99244.84
10	86.37	578.93	841.53	5811.47	99158.47
11	86.88	578.42	928.41	6389.89	99071.59
12	87.38	577.92	1015.79	6967.81	98984.21
13	87.89	577.41	1103.68	7545.22	98896.32
14	88.40	576.90	1192.08	8122.12	98807.92
15	88.92	576.38	1281.00	8698.50	98719.00
16	89.44	575.86	1370.44	9274.36	98629.56
17	89.96	575.34	1460.40	9849.70	98539.60
18	90.49	574.81	1550.89	10424.51	98449.11
19	91.01	574.29	1641.90	10998.80	98358.10
20	91.54	573.76	1733.44	11572.56	98266.56
21	92.08	573.22	1825.52	12145.78	98174.48
22	92.62	572.68	1918.14	12718.46	98081.86
23	93.16	572.14	2011.30	13290.60	97988.70
24	93.70	571.60	2105.00	13862.20	97895.00
25	94.25	571.05	2199.25	14433.25	97800.75
26	94.80	570.50	2294.05	15003.75	97705.95
27	95.35	569.95	2389.40	15573.70	97610.60
28	95.90	569.40	2485.30	16143.10	97514.70

Pmt	Principal	Interest	Cum Prin	Cum Int	Prin Bal
29	96.46	568.84	2581.76	16711.94	97418.24
30	97.03	568.27	2678.79	17280.21	97321.21
31	97.59	567.71	2776.38	17847.92	97223.62
32	98.16	567.14	2874.54	18415.06	97125.46
33	98.73	566.57	2973.27	18981.63	97026.73
34	99.31	565.99	3072.58	19547.62	96927.42
35	99.89	565.41	3172.47	20113.03	96827.53
36	100.47	564.83	3272.94	20677.86	96727.06
37	101.06	564.24	3374.00	21242.10	96626.00
38	101.65	563.65	3475.65	21805.75	96524.35
39	102.24	563.06	3577.89	22368.81	96422.11
40	102.84	562.46	3680.73	22931.27	96319.27
41	103.44	561.86	3784.17	23493.13	96215.83
42	104.04	561.26	3888.21	24054.39	96111.79
43	104.65	560.65	3992.86	24615.04	96007.14
44	105.26	560.04	4098.12	25175.08	95901.88
45	105.87	559.43	4203.99	25734.51	95796.01
46	106.49	558.81	4310.48	26293.32	95689.52
47	107.11	558.19	4417.59	26851.51	95582.41
48	107.74	557.56	4525.33	27409.07	95474.67
49	108.36	556.94	4633.69	27966.01	95366.31
50	109.00	556.30	4742.69	28522.31	95257.31
51	109.63	555.67	4852.32	29077.98	95147.68
52	110.27	555.03	4962.59	29633.01	95037.41
53	110.92	554.38	5073.51	30187.39	94926.49
54	111.56	553.74	5185.07	30741.13	94814.93
55	112.21	553.09	5297.28	31294.22	94702.72
56	112.87	552.43	5410.15	31846.65	94589.85
57	113.53	551.77	5523.68	32398.42	94476.32

Pmt	Principal	Interest	Cum Prin	Cum Int	Prin Bal
58	114.19	551.11	5637.87	32949.53	94362.13
59	114.85	550.45	5752.72	33499.98	94247.28
60	115.52	549.78	5868.24	34049.76	94131.76
61	116.20	549.10	5984.44	34598.86	94015.56
62	116.88	548.42	6101.32	35147.28	93898.68
63	117.56	547.74	6218.88	35695.02	93781.12
64	118.24	547.06	6337.12	36242.08	93662.88
65	118.93	546.37	6456.05	36788.45	93543.95
66	119.63	545.67	6575.68	37334.12	93424.32
67	120.32	544.98	6696.00	37879.10	93304.00
68	121.03	544.27	6817.03	38423.37	93182.97
69	121.73	543.57	6938.76	38966.94	93061.24
70	122.44	542.86	7061.20	39509.80	92938.80
71	123.16	542.14	7184.36	40051.94	92815.64
72	123.88	541.42	7308.24	40593.36	92691.76
73	124.60	540.70	7432.84	41134.06	92567.16
74	125.32	539.98	7558.16	41674.04	92441.84
75	126.06	539.24	7684.22	42213.28	92315.78
76	126.79	538.51	7811.01	42751.79	92188.99
77	127.53	537.77	7938.54	43289.56	92061.46
78	128.27	537.03	8066.81	43826.59	91933.19
79	129.02	536.28	8195.83	44362.87	91804.17
80	129.78	535.52	8325.61	44898.39	91674.39
81	130.53	534.77	8456.14	45433.16	91543.86
82	131.29	534.01	8587.43	45967.17	91412.57
83	132.06	533.24	8719.49	46500.41	91280.51
84	132.83	532.47	8852.32	47032.88	91147.68
85	133.61	531.69	8985.93	47564.57	91014.07

Pmt	Principal	Interest	Cum Prin	Cum Int	Prin Bal
86	134.38	530.92	9120.31	48095.49	90879.69
87	135.17	530.13	9255.48	48625.62	90744.52
88	135.96	529.34	9391.44	49154.96	90608.56
89	136.75	528.55	9528.19	49683.51	90471.81
90	137.55	527.75	9665.74	50211.26	90334.26
91	138.35	526.95	9804.09	50738.21	90195.91
92	139.16	526.14	9943.25	51264.35	90056.75
93	139.97	525.33	10083.22	51789.68	89916.78
94	140.79	524.51	10224.01	52314.19	89775.99
95	141.61	523.69	10365.62	52837.88	89634.38
96	142.43	522.87	10508.05	53360.75	89491.95
97	143.26	522.04	10651.31	53882.79	89348.69
98	144.10	521.20	10795.41	54403.99	89204.59
99	144.94	520.36	10940.35	54924.35	89059.65
100	145.79	519.51	11086.14	55443.86	88913.86
101	146.64	518.66	11232.78	55962.52	88767.22
102	147.49	517.81	11380.27	56480.33	88619.73
103	148.35	516.95	11528.62	56997.28	88471.38
104	149.22	516.08	11677.84	57513.36	88322.16
105	150.09	515.21	11827.93	58028.57	88172.07
106	150.96	514.34	11978.89	58542.91	88021.11
107	151.84	513.46	12130.73	59056.37	87869.27
108	152.73	512.57	12283.46	59568.94	87716.54
109	153.62	511.68	12437.08	60080.62	87562.92
110	154.52	510.78	12591.60	60591.40	87408.40
111	155.42	509.88	12747.02	61101.28	87252.98
112	156.32	508.98	12903.34	61610.26	87096.66
113	157.24	508.06	13060.58	62118.32	86939.42

Pmt	Principal	Interest	Cum Prin	Cum Int	Prin Bal
114	158.15	507.15	13218.73	62625.47	86781.27
115	159.08	506.22	13377.81	63131.69	86622.19
116	160.00	505.30	13537.81	63636.99	86462.19
117	160.94	504.36	13698.75	64141.35	86301.25
118	161.88	503.42	13860.63	64644.77	86139.37
119	162.82	502.48	14023.45	65147.25	85976.55
120	163.77	501.53	14187.22	65648.78	85812.78
121	164.73	500.57	14351.95	66149.35	85648.05
122	165.69	499.61	14517.64	66648.96	85482.36
123	166.65	498.65	14684.29	67147.61	85315.71
124	167.63	497.67	14851.92	67645.28	85148.08
125	168.60	496.70	15020.52	68141.98	84979.48
126	169.59	495.71	15190.11	68637.69	84809.89
127	170.58	494.72	15360.69	69132.41	84639.31
128	171.57	493.73	15532.26	69626.14	84467.74
129	172.57	492.73	15704.83	70118.87	84295.17
130	173.58	491.72	15878.41	70610.59	84121.59
131	174.59	490.71	16053.00	71101.30	83947.00
132	175.61	489.69	16228.61	71590.99	83771.39
133	176.63	488.67	16405.24	72079.66	83594.76
134	177.66	487.64	16582.90	72567.30	83417.10
135	178.70	486.60	16761.60	73053.90	83238.40
136	179.74	485.56	16941.34	73539.46	83058.66
137	180.79	484.51	17122.13	74023.97	82877.87
138	181.85	483.45	17303.98	74507.42	82696.02
139	182.91	482.39	17486.89	74989.81	82513.11
140	183.97	481.33	17670.86	75471.14	82329.14
141	185.05	480.25	17855.91	75951.39	82144.09

Pmt	Principal	Interest	Cum Prin	Cum Int	Prin Bal
142	186.13	479.17	18042.04	76430.56	81957.96
143	187.21	478.09	18229.25	76908.65	81770.75
144	188.30	477.00	18417.55	77385.65	81582.45
145	189.40	475.90	18606.95	77861.55	81393.05
146	190.51	474.79	18797.46	78336.34	81202.54
147	191.62	473.68	18989.08	78810.02	81010.92
148	192.74	472.56	19181.82	79282.58	80818.18
149	193.86	471.44	19375.68	79754.02	80624.32
150	194.99	470.31	19570.67	80224.33	80429.33
151	196.13	469.17	19766.80	80693.50	80233.20
152	197.27	468.03	19964.07	81161.53	80035.93
153	198.42	466.88	20162.49	81628.41	79837.51
154	199.58	465.72	20362.07	82094.13	79637.93
155	200.75	464.55	20562.82	82558.68	79437.18
156	201.92	463.38	20764.74	83022.06	79235.26
157	203.09	462.21	20967.83	83484.27	79032.17
158	204.28	461.02	21172.11	83945.29	78827.89
159	205.47	459.83	21377.58	84405.12	78622.42
160	206.67	458.63	21584.25	84863.75	78415.75
161	207.87	457.43	21792.12	85321.18	78207.88
162	209.09	456.21	22001.21	85777.39	77998.79
163	210.31	454.99	22211.52	86232.38	77788.48
164	211.53	453.77	22423.05	86686.15	77576.95
165	212.77	452.53	22635.82	87138.68	77364.18
166	214.01	451.29	22849.83	87589.97	77150.17
167	215.26	450.04	23065.09	88040.01	76934.91
168	216.51	448.79	23281.60	88488.80	76718.40
169	217.78	447.52	23499.38	88936.32	76500.62

Pmt	Principal	Interest	Cum Prin	Cum Int	Prin Bal
170	219.05	446.25	23718.43	89382.57	76281.57
171	220.32	444.98	23938.75	89827.55	76061.25
172	221.61	443.69	24160.36	90271.24	75839.64
173	222.90	442.40	24383.26	90713.64	75616.74
174	224.20	441.10	24607.46	91154.74	75392.54
175	225.51	439.79	24832.97	91594.53	75167.03
176	226.83	438.47	25059.80	92033.00	74940.20
177	228.15	437.15	25287.95	92470.15	74712.05
178	229.48	435.82	25517.43	92905.97	74482.57
179	230.82	434.48	25748.25	93340.45	74251.75
180	232.16	433.14	25980.41	93773.59	74019.59
181	233.52	431.78	26213.93	94205.37	73786.07
182	234.88	430.42	26448.81	94635.79	73551.19
183	236.25	429.05	26685.06	95064.84	73314.94
184	237.63	427.67	26922.69	95492.51	73077.31
185	239.02	426.28	27161.71	95918.79	72838.29
186	240.41	424.89	27402.12	96343.68	72597.88
187	241.81	423.49	27643.93	96767.17	72356.07
188	243.22	422.08	27887.15	97189.25	72112.85
189	244.64	420.66	28131.79	97609.91	71868.21
190	246.07	419.23	28377.86	98029.14	71622.14
191	247.50	417.80	28625.36	98446.94	71374.64
192	248.95	416.35	28874.31	98863.29	71125.69
193	250.40	414.90	29124.71	99278.19	70875.29
194	251.86	413.44	29376.57	99691.63	70623.43
195	253.33	411.97	**29629.90**	**100103.60**	70370.10
196	254.81	410.49	29884.71	100514.09	70115.29
197	256.29	409.01	30141.00	100923.10	69859.00

Pmt	Principal	Interest	Cum Prin	Cum Int	Prin Bal
198	257.79	407.51	30398.79	101330.61	69601.21
199	259.29	406.01	30658.08	101736.62	69341.92
200	260.81	404.49	30918.89	102141.11	69081.11
201	262.33	402.97	31181.22	102544.08	68818.78
202	263.86	401.44	31445.08	102945.52	68554.92
203	265.40	399.90	31710.48	103345.42	68289.52
204	266.94	398.36	31977.42	103743.78	68022.58
205	268.50	396.80	32245.92	104140.58	67754.08
206	270.07	395.23	32515.99	104535.81	67484.01
207	271.64	393.66	32787.63	104929.47	67212.37
208	273.23	392.07	33060.86	105321.54	66939.14
209	274.82	390.48	33335.68	105712.02	66664.32
210	276.42	388.88	33612.10	106100.90	66387.90
211	278.04	387.26	33890.14	106488.16	66109.86
212	279.66	385.64	34169.80	106873.80	65830.20
213	281.29	384.01	34451.09	107257.81	65548.91
214	282.93	382.37	34734.02	107640.18	65265.98
215	284.58	380.72	35018.60	108020.90	64981.40
216	286.24	379.06	35304.84	108399.96	64695.16
217	287.91	377.39	35592.75	108777.35	64407.25
218	289.59	375.71	35882.34	109153.06	64117.66
219	291.28	374.02	36173.62	109527.08	63826.38
220	292.98	372.32	36466.60	109899.40	63533.40
221	294.69	370.61	36761.29	110270.01	63238.71
222	296.41	368.89	37057.70	110638.90	62942.30
223	298.14	367.16	37355.84	111006.06	62644.16
224	299.88	365.42	37655.72	111371.48	62344.28
225	301.63	363.67	37957.35	111735.15	62042.65

Pmt	Principal	Interest	Cum Prin	Cum Int	Prin Bal
226	303.38	361.92	38260.73	112097.07	61739.27
227	305.15	360.15	38565.88	112457.22	61434.12
228	306.93	358.37	38872.81	112815.59	61127.19
229	308.72	356.58	39181.53	113172.17	60818.47
230	310.53	354.77	39492.06	113526.94	60507.94
231	312.34	352.96	39804.40	113879.90	60195.60
232	314.16	351.14	40118.56	114231.04	59881.44
233	315.99	349.31	40434.55	114580.35	59565.45
234	317.83	347.47	40752.38	114927.82	59247.62
235	319.69	345.61	41072.07	115273.43	58927.93
236	321.55	343.75	41393.62	115617.18	58606.38
237	323.43	341.87	41717.05	115959.05	58282.95
238	325.32	339.98	42042.37	116299.03	57957.63
239	327.21	338.09	42369.58	116637.12	57630.42
240	329.12	336.18	42698.70	116973.30	57301.30
241	331.04	334.26	43029.74	117307.56	56970.26
242	332.97	332.33	43362.71	117639.89	56637.29
243	334.92	330.38	43697.63	117970.27	56302.37
244	336.87	328.43	44034.50	118298.70	55965.50
245	338.83	326.47	44373.33	118625.17	55626.67
246	340.81	324.49	44714.14	118949.66	55285.86
247	342.80	322.50	45056.94	119272.16	54943.06
248	344.80	320.50	45401.74	119592.66	54598.26
249	346.81	318.49	45748.55	119911.15	54251.45
250	348.83	316.47	46097.38	120227.62	53902.62
251	350.87	314.43	46448.25	120542.05	53551.75
252	352.91	312.39	46801.16	120854.44	53198.84
253	354.97	310.33	47156.13	121164.77	52843.87

Pmt	Principal	Interest	Cum Prin	Cum Int	Prin Bal
254	357.04	308.26	47513.17	121473.03	52486.83
255	359.13	306.17	47872.30	121779.20	52127.70
256	361.22	304.08	48233.52	122083.28	51766.48
257	363.33	301.97	48596.85	122385.25	51403.15
258	365.45	299.85	48962.30	122685.10	51037.70
259	367.58	297.72	49329.88	122982.82	50670.12
260	369.72	295.58	49699.60	123278.40	50300.40
261	371.88	293.42	50071.48	123571.82	49928.52
262	374.05	291.25	50445.53	123863.07	49554.47
263	376.23	289.07	50821.76	124152.14	49178.24
264	378.43	286.87	51200.19	124439.01	48799.81
265	380.63	284.67	51580.82	124723.68	48419.18
266	382.85	282.45	51963.67	125006.13	48036.33
267	385.09	280.21	52348.76	125286.34	47651.24
268	387.33	277.97	52736.09	125564.31	47263.91
269	389.59	275.71	53125.68	125840.02	46874.32
270	391.87	273.43	53517.55	126113.45	46482.45
271	394.15	271.15	53911.70	126384.60	46088.30
272	396.45	268.85	54308.15	126653.45	45691.85
273	398.76	266.54	54706.91	126919.99	45293.09
274	401.09	264.21	55108.00	127184.20	44892.00
275	403.43	261.87	55511.43	127446.07	44488.57
276	405.78	259.52	55917.21	127705.59	44082.79
277	408.15	257.15	56325.36	127962.74	43674.64
278	410.53	254.77	56735.89	128217.51	43264.11
279	412.93	252.37	57148.82	128469.88	42851.18
280	415.33	249.97	57564.15	128719.85	42435.85
281	417.76	247.54	57981.91	128967.39	42018.09

Pmt	Principal	Interest	Cum Prin	Cum Int	Prin Bal
282	420.19	245.11	58402.10	129212.50	41597.90
283	422.65	242.65	58824.75	129455.15	41175.25
284	425.11	240.19	59249.86	129695.34	40750.14
285	427.59	237.71	59677.45	129933.05	40322.55
286	430.09	235.21	60107.54	130168.26	39892.46
287	432.59	232.71	60540.13	130400.97	39459.87
288	435.12	230.18	60975.25	130631.15	39024.75
289	437.66	227.64	61412.91	130858.79	38587.09
290	440.21	225.09	61853.12	131083.88	38146.88
291	442.78	222.52	62295.90	131306.40	37704.10
292	445.36	219.94	62741.26	131526.34	37258.74
293	447.96	217.34	63189.22	131743.68	36810.78
294	450.57	214.73	63639.79	131958.41	36360.21
295	453.20	212.10	64092.99	132170.51	35907.01
296	455.84	209.46	64548.83	132379.97	35451.17
297	458.50	206.80	65007.33	132586.77	34992.67
298	461.18	204.12	65468.51	132790.89	34531.49
299	463.87	201.43	65932.38	132992.32	34067.62
300	466.57	198.73	66398.95	133191.05	33601.05
301	469.29	196.01	66868.24	133387.06	33131.76
302	472.03	193.27	67340.27	133580.33	32659.73
303	474.78	190.52	67815.05	133770.85	32184.95
304	477.55	187.75	68292.60	133958.60	31707.40
305	480.34	184.96	68772.94	134143.56	31227.06
306	483.14	182.16	69256.08	134325.72	30743.92
307	485.96	179.34	69742.04	134505.06	30257.96
308	488.80	176.50	70230.84	134681.56	29769.16
309	491.65	173.65	70722.49	134855.21	29277.51

Pmt	Principal	Interest	Cum Prin	Cum Int	Prin Bal
310	494.51	170.79	71217.00	135026.00	28783.00
311	497.40	167.90	71714.40	135193.90	28285.60
312	500.30	165.00	72214.70	135358.90	27785.30
313	503.22	162.08	72717.92	135520.98	27282.08
314	506.15	159.15	73224.07	135680.13	26775.93
315	509.11	156.19	73733.18	135836.32	26266.82
316	512.08	153.22	74245.26	135989.54	25754.74
317	515.06	150.24	74760.32	136139.78	25239.68
318	518.07	147.23	75278.39	136287.01	24721.61
319	521.09	144.21	75799.48	136431.22	24200.52
320	524.13	141.17	76323.61	136572.39	23676.39
321	527.19	138.11	76850.80	136710.50	23149.20
322	530.26	135.04	77381.06	136845.54	22618.94
323	533.36	131.94	77914.42	136977.48	22085.58
324	536.47	128.83	78450.89	137106.31	21549.11
325	539.60	125.70	78990.49	137232.01	21009.51
326	542.74	122.56	79533.23	137354.57	20466.77
327	545.91	119.39	80079.14	137473.96	19920.86
328	549.09	116.21	80628.23	137590.17	19371.77
329	552.30	113.00	81180.53	137703.17	18819.47
330	555.52	109.78	81736.05	137812.95	18263.95
331	558.76	106.54	82294.81	137919.49	17705.19
332	562.02	103.28	82856.83	138022.77	17143.17
333	565.30	100.00	83422.13	138122.77	16577.87
334	568.60	96.70	83990.73	138219.47	16009.27
335	571.91	93.39	84562.64	138312.86	15437.36
336	575.25	90.05	85137.89	138402.91	14862.11
337	578.60	86.70	85716.49	138489.61	14283.51

Pmt	Principal	Interest	Cum Prin	Cum Int	Prin Bal
338	581.98	83.32	86298.47	138572.93	13701.53
339	585.37	79.93	86883.84	138652.86	13116.16
340	588.79	76.51	87472.63	138729.37	12527.37
341	592.22	73.08	88064.85	138802.45	11935.15
342	595.68	69.62	88660.53	138872.07	11339.47
343	599.15	66.15	89259.68	138938.22	10740.32
344	602.65	62.65	89862.33	139000.87	10137.67
345	606.16	59.14	90468.49	139060.01	9531.51
346	609.70	55.60	91078.19	139115.61	8921.81
347	613.26	52.04	91691.45	139167.65	8308.55
348	616.83	48.47	92308.28	139216.12	7691.72
349	620.43	44.87	92928.71	139260.99	7071.29
350	624.05	41.25	93552.76	139302.24	6447.24
351	627.69	37.61	94180.45	139339.85	5819.55
352	631.35	33.95	94811.80	139373.80	5188.20
353	635.04	30.26	95446.84	139404.06	4553.16
354	638.74	26.56	96085.58	139430.62	3914.42
355	642.47	22.83	96728.05	139453.45	3271.95
356	646.21	19.09	97374.26	139472.54	2625.74
357	649.98	15.32	98024.24	139487.86	1975.76
358	653.77	11.53	98678.01	139499.39	1321.99
359	657.59	7.71	99335.60	139507.10	664.40
360	661.42	3.88	99997.02	139510.98	2.98

If we were to consider a $200,000 mortgage (which is closer to the national average of home value) at 6% interest, PI payments would be $1,119.10, and PITI would be $1,626.28. This requires a yearly income of around $60,000 for FHA qualification. With the interest rate being 7%, the PI and PITI consecutively for a $200,000.00 home would be $1,330.60 and $1,838.18 consecutively. A family would need to make $67,000 a year to qualify for this mortgage. Some lenders would increase the term of the loan from 30 years to 40 years or even 50 years to reduce the payment, but the truth is you end up paying more interest in the end.

Lending institution would recapture all of their invested capital in sixteen to twenty years at interest rate ranges from 6%-7%. The family would have paid roughly 29%-48% of the total principal loan balance during the period depicted in figure 5. More than 90% of the PI payment goes toward interest during the first seven years of the loan. At 6% interest, within the first seven years the lending institution would recapture 40% of their total investment while the homeowner would only have paid 10% of the total principal loan amount as demonstrated in figure 6. At 7%, the return to the lending institution would be 47%, while the homeowner has paid 9% toward the principal of the loan.

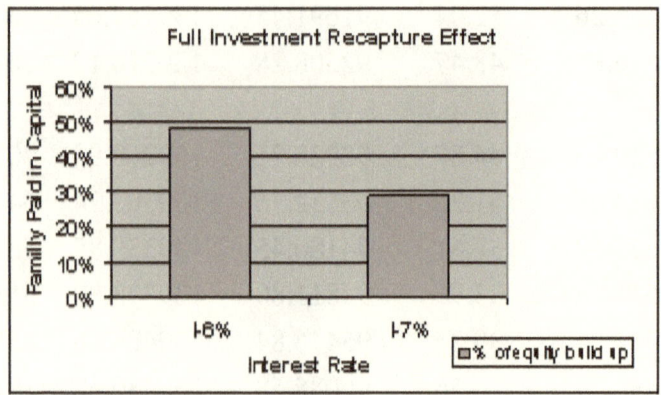

Fig. 4

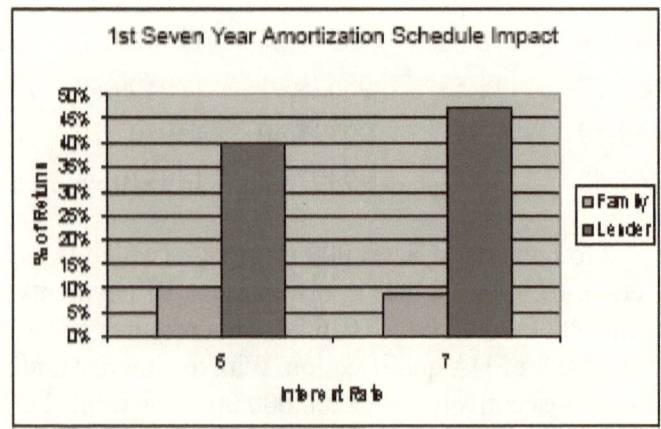

Fig. 5

The market, as it is today without the modernization of the amortization schedule, would undergo a crisis within seven to ten years. In addition, no stimulus package could correct this recession without a real and more balanced amortization schedule. One can easily argue, buying a home does not benefit the homeowner at all, especially when it is kept for seven years or less.

Approximately 90% of almost 31% of our salary is consumed by the mortgage payment, while the other 5% goes toward taxes and insurance. Given current market conditions and the experts' assessment, we do not expect property values to increase by much anytime soon. Based on this assessment, selling a property purchased in today's market within the next seven to ten years will cause serious challenges as it lacks equity.

The current bailout has not benefited the common people. At best it has had a dismal effect. The Federal Reserve has cut the fund rate tremendously and it has nearly hit zero. The U.S. treasury has bailed out the banking institution numerous times in hopes that these institutions will also rescue the homeowners. The bailout loan given to banking institutions was purely aimed at smoothing the progress of assisting homeowners staying in their homes. Fannie Mae and Freddie Mac plan to refinance its borrowers who saw their home values plummet to current appraised values after receiving more than $200billion dollars of aid from us, the taxpayers. We think this plan is far from dealing with the major problem we face. As drastic measures are taken by the government to ensure that lending institutions remain in business, we also think the change we need is to reorganize the amortization schedule, thus creating the savings we can believe in.

If lending institutions agree to adjust the amortization schedule formula where only 75% of almost 28% of our income goes toward the mortgage payment in the first seven years, this would result on a net savings (surplus) to homeowners of 15%. If we really believe this is the worst we've seen since the Great Depression, we cannot expect income to go up anytime soon. In fact, income has already been reduced by employers for most families. Everyone wants consumers to save in these difficult times. One cannot save something one does not have. The current take-home income cannot pay for the most basic bills, let alone savings and investments. To make it through these tough times, debt-holding institutions need to seriously think about taking a pay cut. The mathematical formulas that continue to swing the pendulum one way, especially in this tough economic time, need to be modernized. This will produce a *trickle-up* effect with more money available to save and invest. That is the kind of change we need. This is *real saving*, and that is *saving* we can believe in.

Most of our income has gone into paying debts, so savings will always be hard to come by. The former Federal Reserve Chairman Alan Greenspan reduced the interest rate numerous times; in fact, at one point thirteen rate cuts were done in a losing effort to stimulate the economy. None of this could stop the economy from deteriorating. Now, the government's sole strategy is to create job. Although job creation is germane to this ailing economy, but it is not the whole solution. No number of jobs could ever pay enough money to pay down these consumer debts. Interest rates and jobs are a short-term fix, but the long-term fix is to ultimately unravel the mystery of mortgage debt amortization with more money going toward the principal in the early years. A slight shift of profit sharing could also result in more money in the pocket of the consumers. One can only guess what they would do with this injection of cash. Since we have a lot of smart and innovative people on the shining hill, we can begin to ponder how we can use this cash to build wealth for the people and these countries. No more taxes please!

Everyone seems to have an opinion of the debacle of the market. None cares to mention the impact of the current amortization structure. Some people would tell you despite the imperfections of the system it provides considerable tax benefits to us all. The mortgage interest is deductible; real estate taxes are also deductible. Everyone knows if you have to be offered incentives to make something attractive, then it may not be that beneficial after all. Does the benefit outweigh the cost? Until we decide to commit ourselves to real change, I warn you that history will repeat itself. Some people called it economic cycle. If we knew these days would come, I do not understand why we freak out and spend hours to figure out how we got here. We are in a state of denial. This isn't an economic cycle; this is purely an economic correction driven primarily by greed and crooks orchestrated by corporate giants who ignored all signs to put their interest before protecting our investments.

Chapter 4

RENT VERSUS BUY

Most people would make you believe renting is a bad thing and that you are losing out in the many benefits owning a home offers. Maybe it was so a few years ago, but not anymore. Let's analyze the rental situation today. The table below depicts the advantages and considerations posted in government website Fannie Mae to purchase a home.

	Advantages	Considerations
	Property builds equity	Responsible for maintenance
	Sense of community, stability and security	Responsible for property taxes
	Free to change décor and landscaping	Possibility of foreclosure & Loss of equity
BUY	Not dependent on landlord to maintain property	Less mobility than renting
	Little or no responsibly for maintenance	No tax benefits
	Easier to move	No equity built up
		No control over rent increases
RENT		Possibility of eviction

One of the major arguments against renting is that we are told renters (or tenants) destroy the community because they do not have an equitable interest in the property. If this is really the big anomaly, then I really think we should entertain ways to minimize so-called dysfunctional tenants. One proposition is to consider the creation of a tenant rating system (TRS) where a score is assigned to each tenant available in the tenant database management system (TDMS). One can have an excellent rating for paying rent on time and keep property in the condition received less normal wear and tear. Otherwise, a tenant can be classified as good, fair, poor for any deviation of these principles. The consequence of these deviations is that rent will be increased by a certain factor from the area's normal rent payment. To manage this system, a fee is to be charged to property owners for access to the tenants rating database. We can even take a step further by reporting tenants' delinquencies to the major credit bureaus on a monthly basis. Currently, a good tenant gets a pat in the back, but a poor tenant has their credit ruined with judgments placed on their names, which show up in their credit report.

We can do the same for an excellent tenant. Other proposal is to establish a lending institution for renters, just as we create lending institutions for homeowners. If lenders are worried how they can make money, here is a suggestion. Property owners will require larger deposits from the tenant, which may then be financed by the tenant lending institutions. Tenants can be considered for lower deposits for having a better tenant rental rating (TRR) with longer-term lease. We can also apply the system of leasing where the entire lease is prepaid. This will restore the sense of community we all want in a renter. With all these intricacies also come the need for licensing to ensure proper compliance.

Instead, the government chooses to offer no tax benefits to renters whatsoever. You are literally forced into purchasing a home, or you will suffer the consequence of higher income taxes. This is simply a policy that benefits one group over the other. I believe that renters should be offered the same income tax benefits given to homeowners. So many people now will no longer own a home, and we are left with very few things to write off. Consequently, we will pay more income taxes for seven years or more as our severely damaged credit may take time to improve. In fact, we may never want to buy a house again out of fear of sudden equity loss if nothing is done to level the playing field. Yes, this plan can be achieved and managed.

Presently, the IRS requires only the tax ID and the name of a taxpayer's dependent day care for child-care credit to be granted. The same concept can be used for rental property, where the IRS requires the tax ID and the name of the property owner or Management Company if credit is to be recognized. Think of this, the IRS treats rent collected as income; however, the rent paid is not a taxable deduction. No one conspires to do us harm, but the available options are very alarming and seems to suggest that the system wants to fail us.

Table 1 also shows that when you rent, you have to consider having no control over your rent increase. Although this is partially true, when you buy, you have no control over your tax increase, insurance increase, and maintenance increase. These assessments are not nearly equal, and these tactics are outdated and should no longer be used to lure consumers to becoming homeowner. The home is only yours when you pay it off; otherwise, one should consider oneself as a renter. In one case, the payment goes to the bank with very little benefit to homeowner in the early years and if not paid, the bank can foreclose. Likewise, the rent payment goes to an individual or management company and if not received as scheduled, the renter will be evicted. Also, the home is never yours; the county may also foreclose if real estate taxes are uncollected for many years.

The other consideration of buying a property is equity buildup—this is no longer true. Again, most analysts tell you that home values may continue to decline for a few more years. Let's assume, for the sake of argument, house values remain stable for the next five to seven years or increase roughly about 5%-10%. On Average, a home's repair costs are estimated at about 1%-2% of the property value, there goes the potential equity buildup. I suggest the system should concentrate in savings buildup, via a better amortization schedule. This allows more of the monthly mortgage payment to go toward paying down the loan. This is *savings we can believe in*, not the promise of equity buildup, which may or may not materialize. The risk is too high; we must minimize it through a better mortgage payment structure.

Buy Versus Rent Comparison

The chart below shows a cost comparison for a renter and a homeowner over a seven-year period.

o The renter starts out paying $800 per month with annual increases of 5%.
o The homeowner purchases a home for $110,000 and pays a monthly mortgage of $1,000.

o   After six years, the homeowner's payment is lower than the renter's monthly payment.
o   With the tax savings of homeownership, the homeowner's payment is less than the rental payment after three years.

Years	Rent Payment	Mortgage Payment	Monthly Difference	After Tax Savings	Yearly Difference	After Tax Savings
1	800	1000	-200	-50	-2400	-600
2	840	1000	-160	-10	-1920	-120
3	882	1000	-118	+32	-1416	+384
4	926	1000	-74	+76	-888	+912
5	972	1000	-28	+122	-336	+1464
6	1021	1000	+21	+171	+252	+2052
7	1072	1000	+72	+222	+864	+2664
8-30				*Savings increase every year*		

Monthly Expenses: Buying

Your rental company takes part of your rent payment to cover certain housing expenses. When you decide to purchase a home, you accept responsibility for paying for these expenses (listed below). There are additional costs to the monthly mortgage payment and should be included in the budget estimates:

o   Property Taxes and Special Assessments
o   Home/Hazard Insurance
o   Utilities
o   Maintenance
o   Home Owner Association (HOA) Fee: Doesn't apply to all purchases. It pays for trash and snow removal and maintenance of common grounds if applicable.
o   Membership Fee: It may pay for recreational facilities and other services (cable TV).

The Rent-versus-Buy Comparison table illustrates the dollar benefit of buying a home. This again is very misleading and consequently the less fortunate are being taken advantage of.

The mortgage payment considered drew a comparison with just principal and interest, deliberately leaving out taxes and insurance. Most lenders that will offer you this type of loan today will want taxes and insurance to be included in the mortgage payment. In the case when they are not included, this is still the responsibility of the homeowners. Let's add taxes and insurance to the payment to arrive at a true PITI payment (principal, interest, taxes, and insurance). In this example, a $110,000 home may yield yearly taxes of $1,060 and insurance of $1,800. The monthly PITI payment for this $110,000 property would be $1,238.33. Therefore, as a homeowner you will always be at a net loss for these seven years contrary to what they may lead you to believe. Furthermore, 90% of your mortgage payment goes toward your interest for the first year. In some cases, repairs, association fees, and other fees could bring you even more negative. This is what's wrong with the system: the product can't sell itself, so incentives are necessary to make it attractive. This creates a policy of exclusion. It can be arranged where owning a home can be a viable investment, without the swindle of quick equity buildup. Savings, accumulated by paying down the principal balance with a more sensible amortization schedule, is the real solution. Most Americans sell their home within seven to ten years after purchased. If this trend continues the lending institutions can have a return on investment (ROI) ranging from 40%-61% for interest rates of 6%-9%. In our case, the savings we accumulate during the same period ranges from 6%-12% for interest rates of 9%-6%.

One should notice, the higher the interest rate, the higher the return in investment for the lending institution; and the lower savings for the homeowner. The lower the interest rate, the higher the savings for the homeowners, the lower the profit margin for the lending institution. We cannot afford seven more years of this pandemonium

Lawmakers and their government-sponsored programs may talk the talk of making housing affordable, but that has been done is going the wrong way toward achieving it. For the most part, these programs work in such a way that a homeowner receives grants or bonds to purchase a home and must live in the house for a long period of time (say three to seven years) before they can sell or face the consequence of having to pay back the grant. I welcome these government assistance programs, but we have to continue to be mindful that interests will be paid to the lending institutions during this time of captivity. This ends up making this giveaway very costly to the homeowners. These days, one will be better off saving any minutely accessible money. Maybe the grant money will be better spent making education more affordable for our children and us. Americans can then have a fresh start as they graduate from secondary education.

Chapter 5

CREDIT

Credit Ratings have been a major element to obtain a loan and apply for a credit card, as well as used for many other financing activities. With your credit profile, financial institutions are able to analyze these credit reports and make decisions to extend more credits to you or not to extend credit to you. For many years, the Fair Isaac Corporation credit scoring system has been the model for the majority of financial institutions. This model measures your credit score into the segments shown in figure 7 below:

Payment History	35%
Amount owed	30%
Length of credit History	15%
New credit	10%
Type of credit used	10%

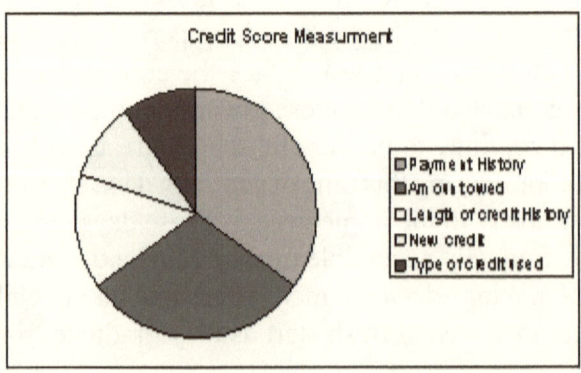

This formula cannot continue to be the standard for this derailed economy. Many people cannot afford most of the things they own. Lending institutions have cut available credit. Employers have cut hours and staff significantly resulting on income reduction or loss of many employees. Consumer credit issues are here to stay and consequential to the current consumer purchasing power or lack thereof.

Day after day, more consumers are delinquent in their mortgages, car notes and credit cards. The generation Y (born in the 1980s and 1990s) may not have a lot of debts and have good credit, but most do not have the income to qualify for these homes and go in a spending spree. College-student futures are looking more bleak than ever as many companies forced to close their doors, making the competition very fierce with an already high unemployed and experienced workforce. Most people just cannot save or earn enough in this economy to buy with cash only. I have personally witnessed the sub-prime market being held responsible for giving out loans to people with very weak credit. The problem is even more complex than we can imagine.

Using the FICO score systems, conventional lenders were turning away many borrowers with excellent credit score. For illustration purpose, a borrower with 680 credit score wants to purchase a home in a decent neighborhood. If this borrower is putting less than 20% down through conventional lending, this borrower will have to pay additional fees like premium mortgage insurance (PMI), as well as the normal PITI.

Now this conventional lending institution may offer an alternative 80/20 mortgage loan program to bypass the PMI, and then the interest rate in the second loan is almost twice of the interest of the first mortgage. The lending institution tells you that because of the risk factor, we need to increase your interest rate in the second loan. The risk is that you are putting very little money down and cannot prove your income despite your good credit standing. In other cases, your credit is not as good; you are putting some money down, and you can prove income. Either case, you are going to be affected with a high interest rate, resulting in a high mortgage payment.

Comparison Table Conventional, FHA, and Subprime

	Sale Price	Loan Amount	Interest Rate	PI	PMI	Taxes	Insurance	PITI
Conventional	$300,000.00	$270,000.00	6%	$1,618.79	$ 203.32	$ 357.58	$ 302.16	$2,481.85
Sub prime	$300,000.00	$270,000.00	7%	$1,887.87	$ -	$ 357.58	$ 302.16	$2,547.61
FHA	$300,000.00	$270,000.00	6%	$1,618.79	154.34	$ 357.58	$ 302.16	$2,432.87

The creditor wins regardless of what you do. The ability of someone to repay their mortgage should not be based primarily on their credit, but rather their income. The current credit system of the Fair Isaac Corporation, also known as FICO, will make it very hard for anyone to purchase a home. Here is our dilemma if we consider theseclasses of people:

- Under seventeen years old: Have very little income, mediocre purchasing power
- Non-college students (seventeen to thirty years old): Credit challenged, limited income and limited purchasing power
- College graduate: Decent and has no credit, has piled student loans, inherited a competitive job market
- Good credit consumers: Most of them won't make any major purchases, besides part of the reason the credit remains so good is their conservatism
- Bad credit consumers: This market is stalled, can't make any major purchases for five to seven years time.

Right now, in this economic climate, we have many people that have their credit impacted and will stay in the sideline whether or not income conditions improve. We can give them jobs; however, they will not be able to make any major purchases due to circumstances that occur over the last few years. This segment of individuals needs to be dealt with. The credit score cannot remain a more prevalent factor in determining what to do with them. The current credit scoring system used by FICO will not work on this frayed economic environment. This means auto sales, furniture and home sales will remain flat for years to come. This will result in home values continuing to deteriorate for many years to come as this inventory sits idle, creating many ghost neighborhoods. We must confront, or bypass, the credit scoring improvement mechanism used by FICO, as detailed below, and deal with these consumer-based issues head-on.

Table: FICO Credit Score Improvement Tips

Payment History

- Pay your bills on time. Delinquent payments and collections can have a major negative impact on your FICO score.

- If you have missed payments, get current and stay current. The longer you pay your bills on time, the better your credit score.
- Be aware that paying off a collection account will not remove it from your credit report. It will stay on your report for seven years.
- If you are having trouble making ends meet, contact your creditors or see a legitimate credit counselor. This won't improve your credit score immediately, but if you can begin to manage your credit and pay on time, your score will get better over time.

Amounts Owed Tips

- Keep balances low on credit cards and other "revolving credit." High outstanding debt can affect a credit score.
- Pay off debt rather than moving it around. The most effective way to improve your credit score in this area is by paying down your revolving credit. In fact, owing the same amount but having fewer open accounts may lower your score.

Don't close unused credit cards as a short-term strategy to raise your score.

Don't open a number of new credit cards that you don't need just to increase your available credit. This approach could backfire and actually lower your credit score.

Length of Credit History Tips

If you have been managing credit for a short time, don't open a lot of new accounts too rapidly.

New accounts will lower your average account age, which will have a larger effect on your score if you don't have a lot of other credit information. Also, rapid account buildup can look risky if you are a new credit user.

New Credit Tips

- Do your rate shopping for a given loan within a focused period of time. FICO scores distinguish between a search for a single loan and a search for many new credit lines, in part by the length of time over which inquiries occur.

- Reestablish your credit history if you have had problems. Opening new accounts responsibly and paying them off on time will raise your credit score in the long term.
- Note that it's OK to request and check your own credit report. This won't affect your score, as long as you order your credit report directly from the credit reporting agency or through an organization authorized to provide credit reports to consumers.

Types of Credit Use Tips

- Apply for and open new credit accounts only as needed. Don't open accounts just to have a better credit mix. It probably won't raise your credit score.
- Have credit cards but manage them responsibly. In general, having credit cards and installment loans (and paying timely payments) will raise your credit score. Someone with no credit cards, for example, tends to be on a higher risk than someone who has managed credit cards responsibly.
- Note that closing an account doesn't make it go away. A closed account will still show up on your credit report and may be considered by the score.

One of the major reasons the market collapsed was because there were not enough buyers with decent credit to continue to buy these overpriced homes. As a result, many lending institutions began to collapse as the market began to shrink. This phenomenon has resulted in a credit shift of the type of borrowers lenders were looking for. By the way, by this time most borrowers with decent credit scores had already purchased a home as lenders shift to make credit a priority—This only makes matters worst. The supply of homes skyrocketed as the market tightens. The demand was there, but lenders became credit conscious, making it hard to sell these homes. As a result, a number of lenders began to slowly disappear, especially the ones that required very little credit for mortgage qualification. Suddenly, Homeowners by the thousands with adjustable rate mortgage could not find lenders still in business willing to refinance these sub-prime mortgage loans. This effect happened so fast for both the lenders and homeowners because so many of us purchased homes around the same period. This was especially true in the community with new construction and condo conversions.

Some statistics may lead you to believe that loan defaults began and were higher with consumers that had very bad credit. Of course this is true, but what the evidence does not show is these credit challenge consumers were paying the highest interest rate in the market. In some cases, lenders were charging 2%-3% interest to borrowers with questionable credit. We all know the income was never there to support these purchases. Then again even if the incomes were there (as paychecks were getting smaller and homes were losing the equity), most borrowers were left with very few options. As always, the less fortunate is first to be impacted.

So in this market, if we are going to create jobs and ignore the credit crisis, many of the people who have seen their credits tarnished by this market will remain in the sideline if we continue to use the same methodology of credit scoring to extend credits to this consumer base.

The FICO system needs to be reevaluated. Credits coring systems needs to be modernized. Most debts are to be forgiven and need also to be deleted from consumer credit reports. We should not have to wait seven to ten years to do it. This economy can't afford this. Morale is low. If we need a drastic change, this is one that will fast-track the economy; as jobs are created, people will continue to use credit again, if given a second chance. Yes, we can. We have given second chances and, in some cases, multiple chances to corporations everywhere. I propose we erase the last few years' credit history and for the government to chip in to help lending institutions recover some of their losses. This credit rating crisis for *us*, the *people*, should be treated as a disaster zone and as such, requires a FEMA-type intervention. If nothing is done to minimize this effect, once people begin to find jobs and make money, I pledge to you lending institutions will be waiting in line to take advantage of their past few years' credit rating to offer preposterous interest rates. We cannot wait for the credit to rebound all by itself in a few years. A word of caution, it may be too late, and we may have set ourselves up for history to repeat itself. Although this is inevitable, the damage can be minimized. Stopping the ongoing credit crunch is in our nation's best interest. This will prepare the next generation of American for retirement.

The conventional way of extending credit to consumers needs a major overhaul. No longer should we allow banks to solicit unemployed and college undergraduates in the manner it's been done in the past. Think about it, the credit card application is too easy to find and requires very little to get approved. I hear most financial advisors suggest to consumers to use credit wisely. This is true in a perfect world. Income is scarce; credit cards are all they have. Consumers will use these cards to the maximum. Mark my words; *you give water to a thirsty man; they will drink it. You give credit card to anyone with no money, and even the ones with money, will use it.* This is money we are talking about; rarely it gets turned away. We know we create this economic mess and there is one other way to get out of it—stop predatory lending. Credit card application should require some sort of employment verification. If credit must be extended to the unemployed, start these credit card users with low limits. Paying on time alone should not be the only factor in increasing limits in a credit card.

Chapter 6

EDUCATION

The education of the next generation of Americans will determine the fate of this country. The United States is a land of opportunity, and people all over the world want to migrate to this country.

The United States is becoming a service state. Foreign manufacturers sell a variety of their products in the United States. Many of the U.S. companies have forced educators and students to focus their study in areas with better job outlooks. As manufacturing jobs are being shipped overseas due to competitive reason (and greed, I might add) more students will select a career to respond with the current demand. The technical skills of a country's workforce are vital to the existence of the country. Otherwise, many Americans in the technical field would have to go to other countries to work or to acquire the necessary skill sets. Yes, we can think global; however, we need to continue to act locally or our dependence will not just be in foreign oil, but knowledge, products, and education, to name a few. We need to seriously consider a change of strategy in the education system to control the exodus of manufacturing job to other countries. Most of the high-paying and stable jobs are in the manufacturing industry.

Manufacturing jobs may be harder to find, but once you have it, it can last for years. Most Asian Americans are in the technical fields. Consequently their median income range is far greater than any other race in the United States. The United States now has a demand for technical workers; in fact, those jobs that cannot be exported have forced companies to import technically skilled workers from other countries to fill these jobs. In addition, these skilled workers require very little training, thus reducing training costs. Yes, we are an educated nation, but one must wonder what skills are we acquiring if we cannot respond to the shortage of the needed skilled personnel. Is it MTV, BET, or Hollywood? Although there is nothing wrong being part of the Hollywood culture, we cannot face the challenge of the next century with this expertise alone. Everyone knows science is already a very difficult subject and one must find a way to excite the young generation to pursue a degree in this field. The curriculum needs to change in high school; more science classes must be a requirement to graduate. The level of math to get a high school diploma right now is dismal, at best. I know we want to offer choices to our kids, but at the same time, we need to control those choices or influence those choices by the kind of curriculum we make available to them.

The situation is pitiful; we are rushing our kids to graduate high school even when they are not prepared. Many of these kids are worried about their grades, not the subject matter. As a country, many of the scholarships are based on grades, not subject difficulty. Most of these students are taking an easy way out. Our influence is bad. We need to rethink how we distribute these scholarship funds. Graduating high school should not be based only in the number of credit hours you have, but also in how well one grasps the subject. In high school, you can have a 2.0 grade point average (GPA) by literally doing nothing. Extra credits alone will get you there. These kids are then attending community colleges around the country, taking classes that are not even college-level classes. Why did we let them graduate if they are taking high school classes in college? Then we sit and wonder why so many kids drop out of college.

These very same kids end up with a pile of student loans, which they may never be able to repay and join the status quo of the dropout club. Guess what, these kids begin to face life with credit problems very quickly as they lack any skills to secure a respectable job with a good salary. And before you know it, they can no longer buy anything on credit. When they do buy on credit, they pay high interest rates, which indebts them even further.

Let's face it America. Some kids are not ready for college. However, do not confuse this with kids who are not meant to go to college. I beg to differ in the former. I believe all kids are meant to go to college and get a good secondary education. We all just can't get there at the same time. Some of us master the material faster than others. This difficulty to learn should be treated as a hiatus, not a showstopper. These students should not be forced into graduating or belittled because they are still in high school at an older age or be sent to an adult education center, which is, to me, like an adult-living community center. We need to create an environment where it is never too late to learn. We should put a limit on students' involvement in extracurricular activities and the social networks. These social networks do boost students' confidence; however, over-involvement can remove them from doing other important related schoolwork. It gets even harder for students who require working after school.

College students that are not prepared for this level and sit in classes with more advanced students find themselves at a disadvantage. So we need to help them learn the basics. Colleges and universities are not the place to teach them the basics. Professors don't have the patience for that, and after all, they may drop out.

Many readers of this book may say, "Where are the parents?" I will tell you, their presence alone can't guarantee the success of these kids. The era we are in, a nerd is becoming something unattractive. You are only needed to do the homework, not to help explain how the homework is done. The muscular guy is the popular one in campus and is the one kids want to befriend. Maybe we should analyze the root cause to the stigmatism toward a nerd and the affection for someone muscular. As the nation transforms in what is viewed to be cool and sexy, the generation begins to embrace it in order to be accepted by others. At this point in time, we can talk all we want about education, but we make other things a priority in our life to the extent we idolize them. The depiction of certain characters in a movie could go a long way to how it influences a generation to come.

The environment we create will have a direct impact in the future generation. We must face it if we want the scientists of tomorrow to come from this great nation, and we need to start acting that way. The TV programs need to embrace it. The government needs to offer scholarships to generate even more interest in science. Then our kids won't just study science anymore just to meet curriculum requirements, but will master it because it is important to their livelihood. Companies are shipping jobs not only because of the cost, but also the skills that come with it. If we want to reverse that trend, we want to give these companies a reason to do that. Our skill levels need to be a force to be reckoned with so that companies don't mind paying us because they will get the productivity and the ingenuity they need from this workforce.

Many in the media will tell you to stop buying foreign-made products as a way to boycott these companies. I have news for you, not only will the trend not stop, but you may not be able to afford the American products anyway. In fact, they may not even be around to purchase. Avoid fanaticism, but understanding the root cause of the problem will serve us better. Fanaticism is only there for a publicity stunt. They come and go very quickly because they are not problem solvers. One can always prefer one thing to the next. These preferences can change at any moment because of an unsustainable foundation.

Many experts are blaming companies for not being innovative enough. We lack behind in the product innovation, and as a result, we are outdone by the competition. I also believe this is not entirely true. Although we need the ingenuity to adapt quickly and build the product of the future, we must be aware of the fact that in the United States we have a saying, "If it ain't break, don't fix it." So we ride the car until it is on empty. In the last ten years, for example, the cultural phenomena were the bigger the car the better it is. While this was very accommodating, it too has a shelf life.

Our system is that we want to take as much juice as we can from any idea; in fact, we want to drain it out without losing a drop. When we stop waiting to be really hungry to look for something to eat, when we stop waiting to be really sick to see a doctor, then we will become a nation that is proactive and not reactive to a problem.

This is very hard for many CEOs to accept or even grasp. They too have a shelf life. Maybe this is where the drainage comes from. Make his or her money and leave the problem for someone else to deal with it. You know, this is very true. What incentives CEOs would have to really invest and commit large sum of capital to R&D to launch a new product? None. Nada. Stockholders can't wait that long. So they ride the wave until it fades away. By then, they will be gone, and most intelligent CEOs would have already made their money. Our society is perceived to be a very patient one, but be mindful, this is just perception, not reality. The reality is we want to make money quickly, so we are very impatient. As quick as it comes it goes.

Education is perceived to be important; then again, it is only a perception. In reality we reward the entertainer, the athletes with big promotion contracts. They become the face of companies around the world. Maybe we can understand why they are the role models of our kids. I want to know if there is something really wrong with these innovators and inventors that we are so shameful to represent the product that they design and build? I believe they are the stars, just like the entertainers and athletes. We just have to make that so. Popularity is earned, not given, so anyone can acquire it if given a chance.

Promoting education in this light will influence the choice of role models for many kids and change a generation forever. They won't just get a job. They will have a decent, stable job that they can rely on through the retirement. For those with entrepreneurial spirit, they won't need to be worried about the most basic knowledge to run a business.

We need education for real jobs, not middleman jobs. Otherwise, we will always be bypassed when things get tough. In fact, As the country becomes more educated, the need for the middleman is tremendously reduced. What most middlemen do is resell access. Access comes and goes quickly. This is why it is not a sustainable economic philosophy. Saving our education system is paramount and drastic measures are necessary if history is not to repeat itself. The continuous stability of the economy is directly proportional with overcoming the educational challenge we face as a nation.

Chapter 7

RETIREMENT

Companies, investors, and lawmakers must understand that retirement cannot be achieved without a better structure of our debts in America. No one should worry if consumers have real paying jobs and savings. The government will not need a stimulus package to entice the economy. The theory spend some, save some, and invest some will be alive and well. The American dream will live continuously, and the roads won't be as bumpy.

Many of the investment instruments lack long-term capital overlay; as a result, they collapse after a period of time. The income structure lagged tremendously as many investments began to outperform, and the wealth did not spread. Profits get distributed at the top tier of the company, and everyone else barely got a raise. When it is to save your income instead of a bonus, you can be sure you will get the pink slip. I am not against top management getting paid for their performance. However, we need to understand making concessions by keeping people employed shares the profit and will help grow the economy. Banks will not have to worry, more deposits and more money will be available to reinvest. In fact, the system barely works when the money is controlled by a few but produced immeasurable results when profits are spread. I wonder which one of those two business models one would prefer to have.

Business Model X: A customer that spends $100 or
Business Model Z: Ten customers that spend $10 each.

I don't know about you, but I prefer Business Model Z. The probability of me losing all ten customers at one time is very slim, so therefore, this business model is less risky. Guess what, most businesses talk the talk but don't walk the walk. We offer reward and incentives to big customers and ignore the small ones. We want to keep big customers as happy as possible. Understand this, it is not good for one customer to have all this say in your business operation. In fact, you will never be able to satisfy that one customer. They then become more of a liability to you.

Now you can see why it is bad when most of the world wealth is in the hands of a few people. These folks control our pay, jobs, and retirements. We can help the government change that by electing people who understand our cause. Many will call this wealth redistribution. This is really a necessary risk control mechanism that removes the focus from the few and place it in the hand of the masses. Focus on more customers, not a few customers to reach real financial stability. There may be benefits focusing in that one customer, but it is risky business in the long term. Maybe you can now see why our markets collapse and our retirement vanished. The investment world is very small, and they all know each other. For us to prevent another disaster, the market needs to be open to many more people. The government should provide incentives to broaden this market and make it more competitive, regulations alone would not stop the market from failing again. When we allow a monopoly to exist, it begins a hazard to our being. We depend on its survival. We can no longer afford a few companies to dominate the market segment to the extent that they cannot fail, and we have to bail them out.

If we want to safeguard our retirement, we should create more competition and ensure that everyone plays by the book. We should stop playing favoritism. Again, the little guy should have a fair share at justice, and we should no longer allow the big guy to buy it. In our society, there are some companies that should shut down for what they do and put their management behind bars, but we cannot do that because they are too big to fail. If we want to get back to fiscal responsibility, the government needs to begin to play its role much better, which is to protect our investments, to shield us against enemy fires. The government should refrain and reduce its involvement into private asset acquisitions because you then become part of the problem. You cannot be impartial, creating conflict of interest. Example, when Fannie Mae and Freddie Mac hold more than half all the mortgages in the USA, it is only fair that the judgments of the government will be obstructed, and the assets of the people will be jeopardized.

Statistics show the economic engine of the American economy is small business. They may not be the highest taxpayers directly, but small business is the largest employer. They are even more fragile to market stigmatism due to their inaccessibility to working capital. They are very susceptible to continuous market contractions. Their voices are not being heard because there are just too many of them to deal with. This is basically inexcusable. Some companies were allowed to be so big that they create a monopoly, and the government is now begging them to stay in business. Some people say these companies are too big to fail, and their failure will create even more problems.

This is very true, but we should never allow ourselves to be so dependent to a few big companies for the survival of the fetus, just like we want to reduce or even eliminate our dependence in foreign oil. Our survival cannot continue to rely in the shoulder of China. We need to start looking elsewhere to create democracy and open our market. It puzzles me how we continue to market our products and create democracy miles away and ignore our own backyard. I am aware that about 60% of the world population lives in Asia, but this should not be the reason not to work with 14% of the population that resides in North America, Latin America and the Caribbean combined. In fact, if we can enhance the standards of living of the Latin Americans, the Caribbean and the North Americans, the immigration problem will be resolved, and the Americas will prosper even more than the European countries.

It is in the United States best interest to create an alliance with this part of the world, create stable government, and improve their standards of living. The logistics will be more plausible for small businesses to expand within the Americas instead of Asia. What we have to see is too quickly many companies take the big cost miles away, and we sometimes have to pay the higher products' cost to recover this big investment. However, closer-to-home expansion will reduce cost tremendously, thereby making products less expensive. As a result, more money is then available to consumers for investments and savings.

The government needs to get back to its core principal, building a just society and provide security to us all. One way to do that is to stabilize our surroundings. Economic opportunity will create stability from stabilized surroundings. When we do that, surrounding countries will not be influenced and take bribes from other countries, making immigrants feel like *real aliens*. We can then begin the gatekeepers of each other. Terrorism will be a thing in the past. Border alliance is long term, but border security is short term. We should work toward a long-term strategy. Alliance is an earned position.

A continuation of the status quo will just repeat this vicious cycle. The lesson learned from the debacle of the world economy is that we have to change course. If government coupled with giant corporations are not willing to participate, we need to take some drastic action to create real savings, thus protecting our retirement and the ones we love. We need to control our debts, spend what we have, not what we will have. To avoid these huge interest charges, we need to pay off and pay down our debts quickly. This will improve our cash flow and create the savings we need.

Chapter 8

BUDGET

Most of us who want to live life within a budget have found it very difficult to do so. Our dreams and aspirations overshadowed any budget plan in our quest to live the American dream. Many of us are going to great lengths to get our kids in the best schools and a safe neighborhood. This premise comes with a hefty price. For the most part, we are willing to live on the edge extending our budget to get that peace of mind and give our kids a chance at stardom.

Safe and good school districts are very expensive to live in. Both mortgages and rental payments are beyond the means of many of us. In fact, home prices in these neighborhoods are even higher than the national average. We talk about how 90% of Americans are making less than $100,000 a year with a median average salary of $43,000 per year. We have also identified most of us would be unable to qualify for $300,000 home. Now imagine how much more the budget is stretched as families and individuals around the nation are looking to be part of these communities. I then come to realize, when we make our kids our priority, *we then do not get to choose our budget, our budget chooses us.*

Most people will tell you, that, if this is the path you choose you should get yourself another job. Indeed, we do; most Americans rely in two incomes to make ends meet. We lead all industrial nations in number of hours worked. I do not know if this is something to brag about or be alarmed about. One could say we are very hard working people. In fact we are, but it has caused us to neglect many other important things in our life. When we are put in a situation to work long hours and sometimes a second job to offer our kids and oneself the type of life we wish, our relationships suffered. We then miss the opportunity to get involved in our kids' life.

We hear very often that the sky is our limit in the amount money one can make. This is very true; however, we tend to see these families very unhappy, as they do not find time to relax and be together as a family. It is very clear that to make money you have to devote the time.

Yes, hard work pays off, but in the process, we can lose everything else. Our society just cannot afford the life we wish without denying our family the bond we yearn. Our budget is dealt with either an increase in income or a reduction in expense. The simple accounting formula is illustrated as follows:

1. Savings = Income - Expense

Or let's look at the other way to match the asset's formula.

2. Income = Expense + Savings
3. Assets = Liabilities + Equity

Let's discuss formula 2 and 3.

In formula number 2, one can argue that you need income to create savings. Also in formula number 3, one also needs assets to create equity. Here is what you cannot realize in formula number 3: without any fault of yours, you can lose all your equity. Most of us work very hard creating assets (real estate, 401(k), stocks, etc.) that will produce the equity we need, also known as net worth. The only problem is when these assets lose their value, they wipe out all our equity, and we are left with the liabilities. If every decade we will go through this economic cycle, then maybe we should risk holding liabilities that exceed a decade. However, if we must invest, there has to be a point we sell these assets to convert the equity buildup into cash or savings.

In formula number 2, this saving is always there as long as you have an income and your expenses are under control. Formula number

2 provides security, but the saving security devalues with inflation. This would not be a problem if income would increase at the rate of inflation because one would be able to save even more, thereby compensating for any inflationary loss. Those who cannot work and reach retirement age should not be affected by inflation by creating the type of incentive that will offset the loss of income. A good example today is the senior citizens community.

One must be made aware of the risk of investing that you can lose the equity as quickly as you build it. Noncash equity is not saving you can believe in because of its dependence on many variables. On the other hand, money put aside after expenses are paid is savings you can believe in. Now one can imagine the importance of living within a budget; one creates the kind of saving that will give you the peace of mind even in a sudden market turmoil. When the market rebounds, many of us will forget these tough times and stop protecting our income. We become complacent and ignore the basic premise of a budget. The more we make, the more we spend. We do not realize you work twice as hard to make what you spend, which means you can lose your income quickly but not the expense. We must be proactive and plan for this difficult time because they will come again. Selling all you have in difficult times to create income is reactive planning; however, saving part of the income you make is proactive planning. I am a strong believer in investing, but one should invest only what you can afford to lose. The rule of thumb should be, "Don't borrow what you cannot repay," subsequently, "Don't lend what you can't afford to lose." This is the only way to create a balance budget that will then produce savings we can believe in.

I strongly believe we need to take matters in our hands and plan for our future; by that I mean one must be proactive. Our savings should be 20% of our income. We are then left with 80% of our income to spend on everything else. So for someone who works consistently for thirty years and saves an average of 20% of their budget every year would end up with 40% of income available to spend every year for a period of fifteen years, if retired after thirty years of working. The major expenditures like homes and cars should already be paid off prior to retirement, which is roughly 50% of our budget as illustrated in the figure below.

Family Monthly Budget

Total Cost	% of income
$8,464	119%

Monthly Income	
Income 1	$4,249.58
Income 2	$2,854.17
Extra income	
Total monthly income	$7,104

Housing	Monthly Cost	% of income
Mortgage(PITI) or rent	$2,699	38.00%
Transportation	$1,350	19.00%
Food Budget	$995	14.00%
Alcohol	$142	2.00%
Tabacco and related products	$213	3.00%
caffeine related products	$142	2.00%
Clothing & related services	$355	5.00%
Life insurance	$71	1.00%
Out of Pocket Health care	$426	6.00%
Investments	$355	5.00%
Etertainment	$355	5.00%
Charitable contributions	$178	2.50%
Beauty products	$71	1.00%
miscellaneous	$142	2.00%
credit cards	$284	4.00%
Social security	$440	6.20%
Maintenance	$103	1.45%
Reading & Education	$142	2.00%
Totals	$8,464	119.15%

Now let us assume that using figure above this family uses the principle of 80/20 budget (saving 20% of income and spending 80% of income). Every year, this family would have put away about $17,000, which equals to over half a million dollars over period of thirty years. If this family lives fifteen years after retirement, then they would have about $34,000 to spend every year. In addition, they can still collect social security. This saving could increase by another 2%-3%, if the government is willing to make it tax free. I assumed salary increases were offset by inflation, so I did not consider it. The assignment of the reader of this book is to take the figure above and first balance the budget then apply the principle of 80/20 budget mortgage lenders in an effort to minimize their risk in a 100% loan. This you receive one loan at 80% and another at 20%. This makes it easier for these lending institutions to sell these securities in the secondary market as they spread the risk.

I know those of us that are affected by the market may not have thirty years to create the kind of savings that produce a decent retirement. These individuals will need to work past retirement age and use a more aggressive principle of 60/40 (spending 60% and saving 40% of their income) in order to accumulate reasonable savings. In the case of two-income family, one income should go to saving and the other should go to spending.

My hope is that we understand the necessity of a budget, and its application will create the savings we can believe in. The bailout is short term, but our saving is long term. We need to create a formula that will produce the savings we need after retirement. A budget is a personal matter and should reflect your lifestyle, not someone else's. Only use someone else's budget as a reference point, but you should never copy it

Chapter 9

PRIORITIES

Every day we wake up and we plan our day. Some of us write down our plan and others just commit it to memory. We set up goals and expectations for ourselves. We contemplate in what is to be the *priority* of that day. So many times, we confuse multitasking for priority. According to the *American Heritage Dictionary*, the definition of priority is (1) precedence, especially established by order of importance or urgency; (2a) an established right to precedence, (2b) an authoritative rating that establishes such precedence; (3) a preceding or coming earlier in time; and (4) something afforded or preserving prior attention.

Priority is a measure of importance, superiority, and first class. It is achieved through the emphasis of what matters most. We throw around the word *failure* for our total disregard to our priority. Our motto in life should be "Goals not achieved are goals delayed." Once we understand this premise, we can now better manage our expectations. We can overcome the obstacles and not let it be deterrence to our priority. The cause of our failure simply ties to being sidetracked in our mission. We must acknowledge this lack of admiration; we must face up to it quickly and swiftly so that goals delayed do not become a second-class goal. We need to understand that inferiority is not superiority and second class is inferior to first class. So many of us fall to second class and accept it for first class. I am here to tell you it is not. Our goals are not shattered until we say so. We may not have control over our destiny, but we should be in control of our priorities. This is again achieved by knowing what matters most to you.

We cheat our kids when we tell them they are the most important things to us; however, our energy, time, and money are then diverted to something else. We work countless number of hours. We are consumed by our careers. We mourn when we do not have money. We won't put off buying the expensive car to ensure our kids go to the best schools. We buy the nicest house to show off to our friends. Most of the time we go out, our kids are not there. These are just not good signs of our kids being our priority. We all need to know putting off something to accommodate something else is not priority. At best, it is a change of priority. In fact, most of your time, money, and energy should be spend in your importance. Maybe it is time to take out the yardstick and measure our accomplishments. How many times do we place second-something that should have been first? Let me count the ways.

We deceive our parents and ourselves when we attend college to obtain a degree; we then come back home with a pregnancy, a marriage, a kid, and all kinds of drama. When you make your education second-class, we should not be surprised when the results are also second-class. Not that I am against these achievements, but we need to understand that there is a time and a place for everything. If you want to do well in school and have a good education, your boyfriend and girlfriend need to come second. I often believe you need to share your priorities with others so you make sure they know what matters to you. Many times this will reveal something very important about the one we hang around with. Not that your priorities should be theirs, but they should respect yours. They should encourage you to achieve them all the time, not when it is convenient to them. On the other hand, we should not impose our dreams and aspirations on others; we should rather share it with them, hoping they can take part in ensuring your success.

Sometimes it is much easier to hang around with people who share a common goal with you. This environment is sometimes less hostile to your needs and wants but could be at times very boring. We have to learn how to balance our time; but many times, we end up with an imbalanced system. We work so hard to make friends, we cheer them, we love them, and sometimes all we get in return is a cold shoulder.

In our relationships, I cannot fathom the possibility of a healthy relationship if we do not recognize each other as a priority. The idea one is receiving more than they are giving sounds very selfish. You cannot tell me you are happy in such a situation.

We all want to be loved and cherished even when we do not express it. Especially when many of us do not master the art of expression, we tend to be very lackadaisical about it. We cannot put off career for someone who will not to do the same for us. We cannot care for someone who does not care for us.

Yes, priorities can change at anytime, but we must recognize that change. We must understand our decisions change our priorities, and that is a mutually exclusive affair. The total disregard for its symmetry can be consequential. This is almost like what is a mother without an infant and what is an infant without a mother. What is a relationship without love and what is love without a relationship? These are the things that nourish our soul, love, relationship, laughter, encouragement, security, etc. Your enemies cannot give that; in fact, you cannot give something you don't feel. I fell short saying you don't give something you don't have, and the reason is very simple, we all have something to share—the question is with who? We cannot save for retirement if we spend everything we have.

Frankly, our retirement is one of the things we do not make a priority, but we think we will deal with it when it comes. Many of us end up being a risky investor and lose everything we have because we never plan for these days, and now we are playing catch-up. We want to continue a lifestyle we did not plan for, and in the process, we risk everything we have, hoping to strike gold. When we mix up our priorities we compromise the outcome., We should not hold others responsible or exhibit abhorrence about someone else's success. This is a matter of personal choice.

I wish I had the silver spoon to everyone's problem including my own, but I can take the liberty of telling you that all roads lead to Rome. Some roads may be less traveled and others may require detours, but we must not let up. We will encounter obstacles in our way that will want to impede progress, and we can go pass these obstacles if we learn how to dump this resistance. Everything looks linear in our eyes, but nothing is. I hope this keeps your expectations in check. I also hope this is the reason we should make plans with what you have rather than what you will have.

There is an old saying that says, "Promises are meant to be broken." Somehow we are at odds when this happens. Of course, it will happen when someone else does not have your interest at heart. No one can manage your priorities better than you. You cannot spend your whole life working for something only to lose it in one day. Whatever you make time to obtain, you must also make time to manage; if not, it will manage you.

The ladder could be catastrophic. We are witnessing that in the financial market. The lending institutions take time to obtain your money, but not manage your money. If they did, I can see how you can be into money management and you failed so miserably at it. The government takes time to occupy our space, not manage our space. When the rhetoric does not match our priorities, we can positively say we are breeding failure. We cannot be bailing out banks and giant corporations and tell me this helps the common people. At best, this is a short-term plan.

We cannot create jobs and encourage me to assume these accelerated interest debts that depleted this income. You cannot tell me to work more when you tax me more. Something I wonder is what makes America great may be what stops it from being greater. The more money you make, the more taxes you pay. In fact, depending on your income, you can pay as little as 10¢ for every dollar you earn or as high as 35¢. If I don't want to pay these kinds of taxes, I am directed into a set of investments that are considered tax deductible and a trap to my savings. This type of tactic does not produce the bailout we need; it only uses up our savings in paying interests. Maybe that explains why we are always a few paychecks away from financial disaster. There has to be a better way to make America great.

I agree steering should be illegal. For those do not know, when a real estate agent steers potential home buyers into buying a home in a community just because this matches your ethnic group, it is known as steering and grounds for license revocation. Nonetheless, when the government steers you into these risky tax-deductible investments that may or may not materialize, it demonstrates a total disregard to our savings and is inexcusable. Hence, this is not the bailout for the people. I want to be clear that I am not against the government collecting taxes; I am just against unfair practices.

I can't understand why I am only able to deduct interest paid on mortgage loans but not the rent paid to my landlord. For instance, if I was in the 35% tax bracket and my mortgage interest was $60,000 for the year, this is roughly a $5555.55 monthly mortgage payment. I will save $21,000 on my federal tax bill. This looks very nice. Meanwhile, in the same 35% tax bracket, the government would return 35% of the 90% of interest I paid to the bank for the first seven years. This I lose 55% of my income to mortgage interest in order to save 35% of federal taxes.

As we know by now, the first 90% of mortgage payment goes to interest the first seven years, so throw away $273,000 in seven years to save $147,000. This is not savings we can believe in. Assuming today's market, as predicted by many economists, remains flat for the next ten years, we will be better offer paying these taxes even with a 5% increase in home value. This will be the right priority to set, but we need the government to share our priorities to make this dream a reality. We don't need handouts; we just want to save more of our money. I know this is going to take some time given the government involvement in the mortgage industry and their stake in the major corporations. These set of priorities should not be placed in the back burner.

INDEX

A

U

W